THE STREETS OF SANTA FE

A Walking Tour from 1880 to the Present

Cover design by Cristina Arnal, Arnal Design, Santa Fe, NM

Maps by Santa Fe Logo Design, Santa Fe, NM

Interior book design by Harvard Girl Word Services, Bandon, OR

THE STREETS OF SANTA FE

A Walking Tour from 1880 to the Present

JOSH GONZE

THE WALKING TOUR

PREFACE

- The Plaza

- Walk west on San Francisco and cross Don Gaspar

- Turn left and walk south on Sandoval

- Turn left (east) on Water

- Reverse direction, walk back on Galisteo, then right on Water

- Continue two more blocks on Water, turn right on Old Santa Fe Trail

- Reverse direction, walk east on Water to St. Francis Cathedral

- Walk to Washington and turn right

- Turn right on Marcy and walk one block

- Continue west on Marcy, then left on Lincoln toward the Plaza

- Turn around, walk north on Lincoln to South Federal Place

- Walk back to Marcy Street, turn right at City HallTurn left on Grant Ave. and walk to Palace Ave., then turn left on Palace

- Walk across the Plaza and down Palace to Paseo de Peralta

- Turn right on Paseo de Peralta, walk to Canyon Road, walk up Canyon Road

- From Christo Rey Church, walk back down Canyon Road 0.25 mile, veer left on Acequia Madre and walk 0.5 mile on Acequia Madre

- When Acequia Madre intersects Paseo de Peralta, walk along Paseo de Peralta

- Turn right on Old Santa Fe Trail, walk to Alameda

- Turn left on Alameda Street, walk ¼ mile along the river to Sandoval Street

- When you reach Paseo de Peralta, turn right and walk toward Community Bank

- Turn right on Guadalupe Street

- Reverse one block on Guadalupe, turn right on Montezuma, walk to Sanbusco

- Enter the Railyard

- Driving down Cerrillos Road

- Driving north on Guadalupe St.

- Driving north on Bishop's Lodge Road

- Driving on St. Francis Drive and the west side of town

- St. Michael's Drive

- Cordova Road

EPILOGUE

FOOTNOTES

SIDEBARS

- Jewish Store Owners

- The first 271 years, from 1609 to 1880

- The Big-Box Store Invasion of Santa Fe

- How Did Santa Fe Architecture Arise?

- Civilian Conservation Corps

- Population of the City of Santa Fe

- Downtown's Filling Stations

- Key Architectural Terms

- Los Alamos

- When Was Paseo de Peralta Built?

- The South Capitol Neighborhood

- The Santa Fe River

- The Automobile Arrives via Cerrillos Road in the 1930s

- The Railroad Arrives in Santa Fe in 1880

- The Interstate Highway

- Special Events: Las Fiestas & Indian Market

- St. Michael's Drive

MAPS

PHOTOGRAPHS

REFERENCES

PREFACE

Prior to the mid-1970s, Santa Fe was a town of bohemians and shopkeepers. There were artists but no galleries. You purchased or bartered for paintings directly from artists' studios on Canyon Road and Monte Sol. For three decades after World War II, no one thought it quaint to shop downtown. It was the only place to buy a work shirt, a refrigerator, or a shoe shine. All three of the city's high schools were downtown. Locals shopped downtown at family owned shops that provided everything from groceries to luggage. There were a few chain stores such as Woolworth's, Sears's, and Levine's, but somehow even the chain stores were infused with local character. Until 1960 there were no street signs in Santa Fe.

In the 1970s the economics of downtown real estate changed. Tourists trod downtown streets on souvenir missions; locals moved south to homes beyond walking distance. Rents rose. Tourist shops could pay higher rent for downtown locations than could old family owned shops. Shops that cater to locals could make more money by moving elsewhere. Shops started closing and by the early 1980s, the gig was up. On May 29, 1983, *The New Mexican* wrote in an editorial, "A person doesn't have to be an old-timer to remember when Saturday shopping meant a trip downtown--not to a mall." Today the chain store invasion that began in the 1970s is still in full force. Independently owned stores are fighting hard to survive downtown but struggling.

Initially I planned only to record the history of what businesses were here before, in the good old days of the post-World War II era. However, I found it necessary to extend back in time as far as 1880, when the railroad arrived, as much of the post-war era cannot be explained without looking further back. The railroad drastically changed Santa Fe and is one of the key events in Santa Fe's 400 years of history. It changed the culture, people, customs, and architecture. It brought painted millwork and bricks to buildings. It replaced the Old Santa Fe Trail, and made it easy to transport large quantities of goods, including perishables such as meat.

This book does not attempt to report every downtown business that ever existed. Instead it attempts to record all those businesses that were firmly established after World War II for a period of at least 10 years and that served as local landmarks.

The book is organized as a walking tour because walking is the only way to truly get to know Santa Fe. If you walk quickly the entire walk takes about four hours. You may begin at any point. There is no need to begin at the Plaza, though it makes a logical starting point.

For future editions of the book, readers may email corrections, additions, and comments to the author at streetsofsantafe@live.com.

DOWNTOWN

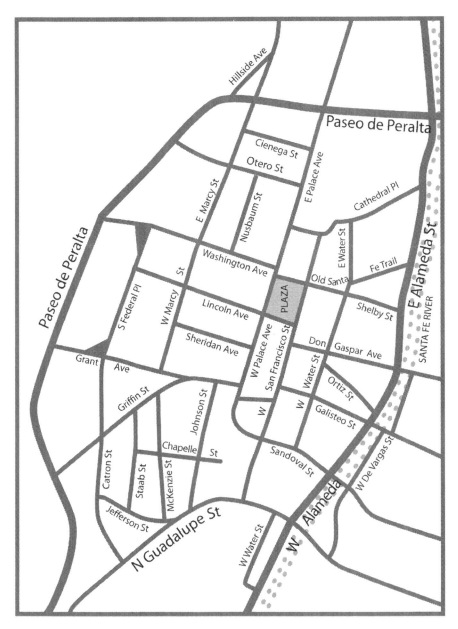

THE PLAZA

The Plaza has been the heart of Santa Fe since it was laid by Conquistador Don Pedro de Peralta in 1609. In the 20th century, until the early 1980s, downtown Santa Fe was filled with stores that served locals. The streets off the Plaza were the center of Santa Fe's commercial life. Shoes, clothing, hardware, service stations, barber shops, and grocers were everywhere. Tourism began changing the stores in the 1970s and by 1985, the year Wal-Mart opened on Cerrillos Road, downtown Santa Fe was a tourist ghetto. Locals no longer shopped on the Plaza.

Locals recall the demise of downtown stores such as Spitz Jewelry (closed 1965), Levine's department store (closed 1971), New Canton Café (closed 1973), JC Penney (moved 1976 to DeVargas mall), Leed's Shoe Store (moved 1977 to DeVargas mall), Capital Pharmacy (closed 1979), Pflueger's Shoes (moved 1979 to De Vargas mall), Dendahl's Fabrics (moved 1981 to Solana Center), Moore's Men's Store (closed 1981), Goodman's Men's Store (closed 1981), Zook's Pharmacy (closed 1981), El Pavon (closed 1982), Plaza Bar (closed 1983), Bell's department store (closed 1984), Kahn's Shoes (closed in 1986), The Guarantee (closed 1988), Veteran's Barber Shop (closed 1990), Dunlap's department store (closed 1990), Sears Roebuck (moved 1990 to Villa Linda mall), and Woolworth's (closed 1997).

Today, only four businesses from the Plaza's heyday remain, three of which cater to tourists: Plaza Café (opened 1905), Packard's Indian Trading Co. (opened 1920), and Dressman's Gifts (opened 1952). The oldest business on the Plaza is First National Bank of Santa Fe (opened 1871).

The Plaza is designated a National Historic Landmark. It looks about the same as it did in the territorial period, from 1848 - 1912. The monument in the center is named The Soldier's Monument. Commissioned by the Territorial Legislature in 1867, the sandstone obelisk honors New Mexico soldiers who fought in the Civil War. It also marks the center of the Santa Fe Land Grant; every property in the city is based on the location of the obelisk.

Begin the walking tour on the south side of the Plaza, which is East San Francisco.

By the late 1800s, the Plaza was busy with retail stores. At that time, a significant portion of that trade was conducted by the five Spiegelberg brothers: Solomon, Levi, Emanuel, and Lehman, and Willi. The first Spiegelberg building, still standing at 72 East San Francisco, was built in 1881. For 28 years, from 1946 through 1974, it was Franklin Women's Clothing, and for 35 years from 1975 to 2010 it was a tourist shop called Simply Santa Fe. (See photo on page 68.)

The second Spiegelberg building, built in 1882, is addressed as 74 - 78 East San Francisco. Today No. 74 is Overland Sheepskin Co. This address was the home of the Moore's Men's Store, owned by brothers Tom and Jim Moore, from 1913 until it closed in 1981.

No. 78 was Spitz Jewelry Store from 1881 until it closed in 1965. Solomon Spitz arrived in Santa Fe in approximately 1880. His son Bernard Spitz inherited the store and operated it until it closed in 1965. The Spitz family still resides in Santa Fe today. The 15-foot Spitz clock stood outside the shop on the sidewalk until 1967, when portals were added to all the buildings on the Plaza. In that year Bernard Spitz donated the clock to the City of Santa Fe, and in 1974 the city installed it on the northwest corner of the Plaza, where it remains today. No. 78 was The Gap from 1997 to 2005, and from 2005 to 2009 a tourist shop called Rodeo on the Plaza.

The building at 80 East San Francisco, the Gans Building, is now a mini-mall of tourist shops. This was the home of Kahn's Shoe Store from 1970 until it closed in 1986. Walter Kahn originally opened his store in 1934 at 127 West San Francisco, then in 1936 moved it across the street to 120 West San Francisco. After 33 years at that location, Kahn's moved to the Gans Building. The Gans building was owned by Harold Gans, known as the "voice of Zozobra" because he performed Zozobra's groaning voice from 1951 to the early 1990s. (See photo on page 69.)

82 East San Francisco was Capital Pharmacy, which closed in 1979. Capital Pharmacy had a soda fountain with 12 tables that was a popular gathering place for students from nearby St. Michael's High School and Loretto Academy. Capital traced its origin to the A.C. Ireland Pharmacy, founded in 1888, which moved to the Plaza in 1905 and changed its name to Capital Pharmacy in 1909. The corner location at 84 East San Francisco was Leed's Shoe Store, which moved to DeVargas Center in 1977 and later closed.

In the center of the block is an indoor mini-mall called Plaza Galleria. This was the old JC Penney, with the address of 66 - 70. (See photo on page 67.) When JC Penney moved to DeVargas mall in 1976 (where Office Depot is today), it was replaced on the Plaza by Dunlap's department store. (In 1976 Dunlap's moved from the location that is today's Santa Fe Dry Goods). Dunlap's closed in 1990. In 1991 - 92 the former Dunlap's/ JC Penney building was gutted and replaced with Plaza Galleria, a disappointing blur of dull tourist shops.

F.W. Woolworth's & Co., a variety store, was on the south side of the Plaza from 1935 until the demise of the entire Woolworth's chain in 1997. When Woolworth's closed in 1997, it was the end of the era. In its place, an independent store called Five & Dime General Store took over a quarter of its space and still operates today, principally serving tourists. In 1999, the Historic Design Review Board approved a proposal to redesign the front façade of the old Woolworth's. Three-fourths of the old Woolworth's was razed, a new interior wall was constructed to wall off the new Five & Dime, and the newly cleared space was replaced with a three-story indoor mall called Santa Fe Arcade, which opened in 2004. (See photo on page 70.)

Now shift to the east side of the Plaza, looking at the Catron Building, built in 1890. The corner location, now Santa Fe Dry Goods, has always been a clothing store. In the early 20ᵗʰ century it was called The White House. In the 1940s the location became Hinkel's, which was succeeded by Hubbard's in the mid-1950s. In the 1960s, Dunlap's replaced Hubbard's. Dunlap's relinquished the space to The Guarantee in 1976 when Dunlap's moved into the former JC Penney location on the south side of the Plaza. The Guarantee, owned by Marian and Abe Silver, was among the last of the retail shops for locals when it closed in 1988. Note that the ground floor is labeled The Silver Building, a reflection back in time to The Guarantee.

To the south of The Catron Building is today a tourist shop called Lucchese Boot Co. The building was originally a majestic Greek Revival building built in 1912 for First National Bank of Santa Fe, with tall stone columns. In 1954 the columns were removed, the entire front wall of the building was replaced with glass, and it became Levine's department store. The bank moved across to the northwest corner of the Plaza, where it remains today. Levine's closed in 1971 and the huge glass wall was covered with stucco.

Today, at the corner location is Packard's Indian Trading Co., which has been in Santa Fe since 1920. From 1956 to 1982, the corner was El Pavon, a clothing store. Prior to 1982, Packard's was in between El Pavon and Levine's. When El Pavon closed, Packard's knocked down the wall and expanded into its space. Prior to 1956 when El Pavon opened, the corner was occupied by the Railway Ticket Office, where passenger tickets could be purchased for the railroad. The Ticket Office was built in 1926 by William Penhallow Henderson, an artist and architect who was a key force for Spanish-Pueblo Revival in the early 20ᵗʰ century. In the mid-1990s, Toltec Builders Inc. restored it to its 1925 appearance.

At the southeast corner of the Plaza is La Fonda hotel, which opened in 1922. The site has been occupied by a series of hotels since Santa Fe's earliest days in approximately 1607. From 1833 to 1837 it was a hotel called The U.S. Hotel. From 1837 to 1848 it was a hotel called La Fonda, a name that was resurrected in 1922. From 1848 to 1867 it was (for the second time) called The U.S. Hotel. It was sold in 1867 and renamed The Exchange Hotel, which it remained until 1919. The Exchange was razed in 1919 and today's La Fonda was built. In 1925 the Atchison, Topeka, and Santa Fe Railroad purchased the hotel and leased it to Fred Harvey Company, which was engaged in hotels and tourism in the west. From 1925 to 1969 La Fonda remained part of the Harvey Houses, a chain of western tourist hotels. In 1968, La Fonda, then in disrepair, was sold to Sam Ballen for $1.5 million. Ballen restored it and owned it until his death in 2007. (See photo on page 71.)

Now cross to the west side of the Plaza. The corner building was built in 1976 to replace the prior building, which was destroyed by fire in early 1976. The building owner, Armand Ortega, hired architect Bill Lumpkins to design a new building based on a photograph of a building that had stood on the site back in 1878. Armand Ortega has been an important merchant on the Plaza since that time and now owns three businesses on the Plaza: Ortega's, Yippee Yi Yo, and Mimosa. Ortega's has been in the corner building since it was constructed in 1976. The upstairs was The Ore House Restaurant for 34 years, from 1976 to 2011.

Plaza Café has been in business since 1905 at this location. Next door to the Plaza Café there was a bar called the Plaza Bar, which closed in 1983. It is now a tourist shop called Plaza West Trading Co. Plaza Café and Plaza Bar were connected inside. You could order food at the café and take it into the bar. It was a dive bar, filled with blue collar folks, artists, writers, and everyone else except the upper class.

The northwest corner has been First National Bank of Santa Fe since 1954. The building dates to the early 1920s and was constructed in Spanish-Pueblo Revival as El Oñate Theater, a movie house, on the site of the 19th century Capital Hotel. The theater's building also contained an auto dealer ship and a retail store. The theater lasted only four years before closing in 1924 and its space was used for retail shops until the bank acquired the building.

Now return to the south side of the Plaza. Zook's Pharmacy was in the building now home to Plaza Bakery, often called Haagan Dazs because of the large ice cream sign. Zook's was opened by John Zook in 1908. When he died in 1950, his daughter Katie took over and ran it until her retirement in the 1970s. Zook's had a 14-seat lunch counter, the last of its kind in Santa Fe. Zook's closed in 1981 and Plaza Bakery replaced it the same year. A book published in 2011, E. B. Held's *A Spy's Guide to Santa Fe and Albuquerque*, made the case that Zook's figured in the assassination of Leon Trostsky in 1940 in Mexico City. According to the book, a KGB agent had an affair with Katie Zook and used Zook's to plan the assassination. (See photo on page 72.)

The tourist shop called Yippee Yi Yo is at 54 East San Francisco. This was Kaune's grocery store until 1955, when it closed this location and expanded to two larger locations: In 1955 at the corner of Paseo de Peralta and Old Santa Fe Trail (then Manhattan and College Streets), and in 1956 at 208 Washington (now Washington Federal Bank). Kaune's grocery stores have been in Santa Fe since Harry S. Kaune opened the original store in 1896 on the Plaza at 104 West San Francisco (now the Nambe shop). Later it moved to 54 East San Francisco. Back in the old days, Kaune's had its own bakery that people loved. "Brownies, cupcakes, pecan pies. It broke my heart when they shut down the bakery," said one sad former customer.

JEWISH STORE OWNERS

Starting in the 1880s, Jews have had a cultural and business presence in Santa Fe. Many of the early merchant families were Jewish, including the Speigelberg, Spitz, Ilfeld, Staab, and Seligman families. Until the 1970s, Jewish shopkeepers remained in business downtown. Marion and Irving Bell owned Bell's department store, which had been opened by Irving's father Morris in 1926. Walter Kahn owned Kahn's shoes, which had been opened by Walter's father Gus Kahn in 1934. Abe and Marion Silver, with Marion's brother Gene Patchesky, owned The Guarantee. Mendel Goodman opened Goodman's in 1929 and passed the store on to his son Morey Goodman. And there were many more.

As a symbol of Jewish financial contributions to the construction of St. Francis Cathedral and the strong bond between the city's Catholics and Jews, the Hebrew inscription for God decorates the main entrance and there are two six-pointed stars inside, one visible from the pulpit and another visible in the vestuary. Monsignor Jerome Martinez y Alire wrote about the Hebrew inscription: "Because they (the city's Jews) later forgave the debt, it is held that the tetragram carved in the archway over the Cathedral's main door indicating the Hebrew name for God was Lamy's way of thanking them. As my mother would have said, "If the story's not true, it should be.""[1]

Similarly, at Holy Faith Episcopal Church, the glass above the main entrance contains a Star of David. This church was founded in 1863, shortly before the Presbyterians founded First Presbyterian Church in 1867.

Walk west on San Francisco and cross Don Gaspar

Get your bearings: East of Don Gaspar Ave., San Francisco St. is *East* San Francisco. West of Don Gaspar Ave. it's *West* San Francisco.

For more than 50 years, West San Francisco housed several numerous businesses that everyone knew.

Begin with the left-hand (south side) of the street. Goodman's Men's Store, which opened in 1929 and closed in 1981, was on the corner at 100 West San Francisco, which today is Fisher Fine Pottery. In 1910, Pflueger's Shoe Store opened at 106 ½ West San Francisco (now Starbucks). In 1979 Pflueger's moved to the DeVargas mall, then to Villa Linda mall, and now is no longer in business.

Today the addresses 112 to 118 belong to Plaza Mercado, a three-story indoor mall with entrances on San Francisco and on Water. This building was constructed in three phases from 1985 to 1990 by Gerald Peters, a local property owner. Previously the site of Plaza Mercado was three buildings that were home to Elliot's 98-Cent Store, Payless Drug Store, and Bell's department store. 112 had been Taichert's Variety, which changed its name to Wacker's Variety in the 1960s and then to Elliot's 98-Cent Store in the 1970s. 114 was Payless. 116 was Bell's, which remained open for 60 years before closing in 1984. Gerald Peters demolished the old buildings in 1984.

No. 120, now a tourist art gallery, was Kahn's Shoes from 1936 to 1970, when it moved up the street to 80 East San Francisco.

The corner building at 122 West San Francisco was a women's clothing shop called La Tienda, which is often credited with being the spark that got women interested in Santa Fe style, Indian-inspired clothing of the southwest. La Tienda was at that location from 1929 to 1981. Today that address is Chico's, a national chain of women's clothing stores.

A stone plaque at the corner of West San Francisco and Galisteo survived Plaza Mercado and reads:

1923
N.B. Laughlin
Owner
C.M. Campbell
Builder

N.B. Laughlin was the maternal grandfather of Laughlin Barker (1921-2011), a prominent real estate broker and builder in Santa Fe for decades, whose son David Barker owns Barker Realty today.

Now look at the right-hand side (north side) of the street. In the 1950s, at 121 there was Mitchell's music store, owned by Gus Mitchell, which today is Parts Unknown. Gus Mitchell also owned Mitchell's Army & Navy Store at 205 West San Francisco, which is now Moxie gift shop. Both locations have hosted a series of forgettable businesses over the subsequent years.

Next was the El Paseo theater, which today is Coldwater Creek. Santa Fe's first movie house, The Paris, opened at this location in 1913. It remained open until it was destroyed by fire in the late 1940s. It was rebuilt as the El Paseo movie theater, which was open from 1951 to 1972, then again from 1983 to 1985. Its classic movie marquee was a symbol of downtown Santa Fe. From 1972 to 1983 and from 1985 to 1992 the site was vacant. When the El Paseo closed in 1972, it was because its owner, Commonweath Theaters, had opened a new twin-screen theater called the Coronado Twin at the east end of the Cordova Road shopping center. In 1992 the building was renovated and became a Banana Republic clothing store. In 2006 Banana Republic closed and was replaced by Coldwater Creek. (See photo on page 73.)

After the El Paseo, at 125 there was New Canton Café, a Chinese restaurant, which was open from 1922 to 1973. In 1975 Tia Sophia's opened in the space that had been New Canton Café. In 1982 Tia Sophia's moved across the street to its present location at 210. Today the former site of Tia Sophia's is a rug merchant.

Two doors down at 129 was Dendahl's Fabrics, now an indoor mini-mall (the street addresses were modified slightly in the 1980s, so 129 no longer corresponds to that mini-mall). Dendahl's was owned by the Dendahl family, whose son John Dendahl was chairman of the New Mexico Republican Party from 1994 to 2003. Dendahl's moved to Solana Shopping Center on West Alameda in 1981 and later went out of business. Next was Candelario's Curio Store, which has been there since around 1903.

On the corner of Galisteo is Evangelo's Cocktail Lounge. The bar was opened in 1969 by Evangelo Klonis, a Greek immigrant who for thirty years beginning in 1936 had owned and operated The Mayflower Café on the south side of the Plaza. (See photo on page 68.)

The corner location of Evangelo's was for many years it was a soda fountain called Faith Café. Faith Café was operated by a Greek family with the surname Kalangis. Faith Café was destroyed by a fire in 1967. Ike Kalangis, son of the proprietors of Faith Café, was later CEO of Sunwest Bank.

From 1924 to the 1980s, Livingston Furniture, owned initially by Hyman Livingston, was at 204 West San Francisco. Now that address belongs to a touristy art gallery. Livingston Furniture moved to DeVargas Center in the 1980s, then to Villa Linda mall, and it closed in 2000. The painted billboard for Livingston Furniture remains visible on the exterior bricks of the second story.

208 West San Francisco, now a trinket shop called Ritual Adornments, was Collected Works bookstore for 31 years, from 1978 to 2009. In that year it moved to its present location at 202 Galisteo St.

207 West San Francisco, now a restaurant called Burro Alley Café, which opened in 2010, was a family owned grocery called City Cash Market in the 1940s and early '50s. In the early '50s it became a lunch counter called Ross's Cafeteria. In the 1965 the site was taken by a popular restaurant called Raul's Café, which lasted 26 years and closed in 1981.

In the 1880s, the site on San Francisco that is now Tia Sophia's Restaurant and the Sandoval Street parking garage was a two-story hotel called Herlow's Hotel. In 1938 - 39 Salmon and Greer (builders of the Lensic) purchased the site, razed the hotel, and built the beloved Burro Alley Theater, better known simply as The Alley, at 212 West San Francisco. The Alley opened in 1939, closed in 1968, and its building was later razed. The parking garage was built in 1988.

In 1930, Nathan Salmon and his son-in-law, John Greer Sr., announced plans to build a large, elaborate movie theater, the first of its kind in Santa Fe. The Lensic Theater opened in 1931. The architect of its pseudo-Moorish design was Boller Brothers of Kansas City, a vaudeville house architect that designed almost 100 theaters in the west and Midwest, including the KiMo in Albuquerque. The name Lensic derives from the initial letters of Greer's six grandchildren. In its glory days, stars like Roy Rogers, Errol Flynn, Ronald Reagan, Rita Hayworth, and Judy Garland appeared there. By the 1980s it had become seedy but it remained open until 1999. It closed for renovation and re-opened in 2001 as a performing arts venue. Inside the theater has 843 seats imported from Colombia and murals with scenes from both local history and imagined Arabian palaces.

Burro Alley is a reminder of the centuries during which burros walked Santa Fe's streets, carrying firewood, sacks of grain, or anything else that a packer could rope to the animal's back. Santa Fe's last working burros disappeared in the 1930s. Today Burro Alley has a statue of a burro to recall the contribution these animals made for more than 300 years.

Square Deal Shoe Shop, which is still in operation on St. Michael's Drive, was opened in 1928 on Burro Alley by Manual Gallegos. It was there until 1985, when it moved to Johnson Street. In 1995 it moved to St. Michael's Drive, where is still run today by David Gallegos, the son of Manual. Square Deal was next door to Veteran's Barber Shop at 32 Burro Alley. Veteran's opened in 1952 and closed in 1990. The owner, Joe Gonzales, cut hair at that location for 38 years.

Now walk past the Lensic to the corner. Prior to about 1972, McMurtry Paint Store was located at 225 West San Francisco, which is now a parking lot. The building was razed around 1972 to allow for the construction of Sandoval Street. Previously, that portion of Sandoval Street did not exist. It was buildings and a parking lot in back. McMurtry Paint was purchased by Joe Valdes in 1972. He changed the name to Valdes Paint and Glass and moved it to Early Street. He served as mayor of Santa Fe from 1972 to 1976. In 2008 the Early Street location closed and the business consolidated with Valdes Picture Frames and Art Supplies, around the corner on Marquez Place.

The two-acre site on West San Francisco where the Eldorado Hotel stands was a lumber yard called Big Jo Lumber from 1927 to 1983. In the 1850s, on the same site, previous to Big Jo Lumber, there was a hotel by the same name--Eldorado Hotel. In 1983 the site was purchased by Nancy and Bill Zeckendorf, and in 1985 the Eldorado Hotel opened. In 1986 Big Jo Lumber re-opened on Siler Road as Big Jo Hardware. The 12,000 square foot building on Siler Road had formerly housed a moccasin factory and then, in the 1970s, a roller disco rink.

The First 271 Years, from 1609 to 1880

Santa Fe was founded in 1609 by Pedro de Peralta as the northernmost province of New Spain. Beyond that, it was pioneered and built by a small number of Spanish-Indian families who came north from Mexico in 17th, 18th, and 19th centuries. Their poetic surnames are still common in Santa Fe today: Roybal, Ortiz, Pacheco, Adelo, Armijo, Romero, C de Baca, Lovato, Archuleta, Gallegos, Quintana, Vigil, Trujillo, Candelaria, Montoya, Cordova, Delgado, Garcia, Jaramillo, Aragon, Gonzales, Rodriguez, Martinez, Hernandez, Valdez, Ortega, Segura, Herrera, Lujan, Sena, Salazar, Apodaca, Anaya, Sandoval, Bustamante, Tapia.

Until 1846 the city was linked to Mexico City by 1,600 miles of El Camino Real (The Royal Road). The last stop on El Camino Real before reaching Santa Fe was a ranch that remains in existence as a historic living ranch, Las Golondrinas, which is located about 10 miles to the south of downtown Santa Fe.

In 1829 a new trail, called the Old Spanish Trail, linked Santa Fe to California, which was then also part of Mexico. Trading caravans were the predominant users of these trails.

On August 18, 1846, in an early period of the Mexican-American War, an American army general, Stephen Kearny, occupied Santa Fe and raised the American flag over the Plaza. The result was that The Santa Fe Trail replaced El Camino Real as the principal path to Santa Fe. The Santa Fe Trail was a 900-mile wagon road that linked Missouri and Santa Fe beginning in 1821, the year Mexico became independent of Spain. In 1846 it became the primary road to Santa Fe, a role it served until the railroad arrived in 1880.

Gen. Kearny ordered the construction of Fort Marcy, just north of downtown Santa Fe, for the defense of Santa Fe. It was constructed on the hill where the Cross of the Martyrs is today. The fort was never needed and it closed in 1891. Marcy Street runs along the edge of the former Fort Marcy. Kearny Street, named for the General, is a small residential street on the hill where the fort stood.

In 1848, by the Treaty of Guadalupe Hildago, the U.S. acquired the land encompassing what is now New Mexico and the New Mexico became a U.S. Territory. The cession that the treaty facilitated included parts of the modern-day U.S. states of Colorado, Arizona, New Mexico, and Wyoming, as well as the whole of California, Nevada, and Utah. The remaining parts of what are today the states of Arizona and New Mexico were later ceded under the 1853 Gadsden Purchase.

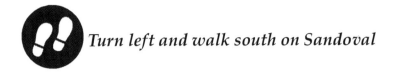 *Turn left and walk south on Sandoval*

The Hilton Hotel opened in 1972 on a site previously known as Five Points because five streets intersected there (Alameda, Water, Sandoval, San Francisco, Agua Fria). At the middle of the intersection, at the location of what is today a bank, was a small island with a liquor store known as Five Points Liquor. The building facing Sandoval (what is now the front of the Hilton) was Montoya Furniture. The largest building on the site, facing Guadalupe, was the Electric Laundry, a commercial laundry that started in 1912 and was owned for decades by the Koch (pronounced Cook) family. In 1968 the Santa Fe River flooded and damaged many of the buildings in Five Points, which led to their demolition and the subsequent construction of the Hilton.

First Northern Plaza, a retail/office building at the southeast corner of Sandoval and Water, was built in 1969 - 70, another consequence of the 1968 flood.

THE BIG-BOX STORE INVASION OF SANTA FE

- Kmart in 1976

- Wal-Mart in 1985 at its original location which closed in 1994, now Office Depot at 2016 Cerrillos Road.

- Wal-Mart in 1994 at its current location, the former Pueblo Drive-In, at 3251 Cerrillos Road

- Sam's Club in 1993

- Target in 1999

- Whole Foods in 2000

- Home Depot in 2000

- Lowe's in 2007

- Kohl's in 2007

- Buffalo Thunder Resort in August 2008

- REI and the Railyard in September 2008

- Santa Fe Convention Center in September 2008

- Super Wal-Mart in October 2011

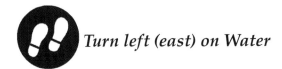 *Turn left (east) on Water*

In the 1950s and early '60s, Tiny's Bar and Lounge was a storefront bar downtown at 125 W. Water, directly across from the bus station. In 1961 it moved down the street to 221 W. Water, which is the site of Sandoval Parking Garage. In 1971 Tiny's moved to its present location in Crossroads Center.

Pause at the corner of Water and Galisteo. The three-story building at 202 Galisteo that houses Collected Works bookstore was constructed in 1923 as a hotel called El Fidel Hotel, which lasted for nearly 50 years. In 1973 the building was acquired and renovated by First Northern Savings and Loan, according to a plaque in the entry. From 1973 to 1989, the ground floor was The Winery, a deli/wine bar/wine shop. From 1989 to 2009, it was Foreign Traders. Collected Works moved into the building in 2009 after 31 years in business at 208 West San Francisco.

A plaque on the side of the former El Fidel Hotel marks the location of the Santa Fe County Jail where William "Billy the Kid" Bonney was held from Dec. 27, 1880, to March 28, 1881.

Looking left on Galisteo, there was The Old Mexico Shop, a warehouse store opened in 1927 by Tony Taylor, the brother of Ladybird Johnson, who was the wife of President Lyndon Johnson. Its two entrances were at 123 Galisteo and 141 West Water. Old Mexico Shop was the first store in Santa Fe to import large volumes of Mexican goods such as sandals, tile, glass, furniture, and crafts. In the 1980s, Tony Taylor's grandson, Alexander Tschursin, took ownership of the Old Mexico Shop. In 1989, when the third and last phase of Plaza Mercado was built, The Old Mexico Shop changed its name to Foreign Traders and moved to 202 Galisteo (now Collected Works), where it remained for 20 years until its closure in 2009.

The Old Mexico Shop was in the old Charles Ilfeld Co., the city's largest dry goods store in the late 19th century. Charles Ilfeld was a German Jewish merchant who arrived in Santa Fe in 1865 and died in 1929. In 1989, the Ilfeld building was renovated to build Plaza Mercado. The former storefront of Old Mexico Shop is no longer recognizable, though its painted brick front wall facing Galisteo was preserved when the building was gutted.

Now look at the corner building at 124 Galisteo. In the 1940s and '50s, this was a raucous bar known as George King's Bar, though its official name was King's Blue Canteen. Artists Alfred Morang and Will Shuster would drink at George King's, and Shuster did a painting of a typical night there. In its November 12, 1967 edition, *The New Mexican* described the painting as: "A blind female violinist, a piano player with no legs, wooden floors that bounced with dancing bodies or knocked-out bar fighters, this was the atmosphere in George King's Blue Ribbon Bar." The bar closed in 1961.

Katty-corner to the former George King's Bar, there is a small furniture store called Sequoia. In the 1980s, this was the location of Downtown Subscription, a popular coffee shop that moved to the old Tito's Market location at 376 Garcia in 1990. In the 1950s and '60s, this location was Paul Ragle's filling station. Ragle Park, a city-owned park on Rodeo Road, is named after Paul Ragle. Ragle was one of the founders of the Santa Fe Rodeo, which originally occupied the site that became Ragle Park.

Now walk down Galisteo for one block. The store at 222 Galisteo (now vacant) was Artisanos Imports from 1965 until 2006. The owner, Polo Gomez, had spent 11 years prior to 1965 working at The Old Mexico Shop. After learning the business there, he opened Artisanos. Artisanos is still in business at 1414 Maclovia, off Cerrillos Road, and is run by the children of Polo Gomez.

Until the mid-1980s, the site of Seret and Sons at 230 Galisteo was Tiano's Sporting Goods, owned by the Tiano family. The upstairs of Tiano's was a small, cheap hotel called the Hope Hotel with approximately six or eight rooms. Some locals recall the Hope Hotel was a bordello.

From 1961 to 1982, the Senate Lounge was a lively bar with a sunken dance floor at 221 Galisteo, across from Tiano's. Yellow Page ads for the Senate Lounge said "Dining, Dancing, Orchestra." In the mid-70s, it became a strip bar until that form of entertainment was prohibited by a city obscenity ordinance. On January 30, 1975, *The New Mexican* reported "Two topless dancers and the owner of the Senate Lounge were arrested on charges of indecent exposure and lewd and indecent behavior by Santa Fe detectives." In its later years, the Senate Lounge was a gay and lesbian bar. "It was a real scene," recalled one old-timer. "You never knew which bathroom to go into."

Around the corner on West Alameda St., from 1981 until 1991, a music and dance club called Club West was located at 213 West Alameda, between Sandoval St. and Galisteo St. It was a cavernous black room jamming with loud music. The building is now the back building of Seret and Sons.

How Did Santa Fe Architecture Arise?

Santa Fe's distinctive architecture exists in two styles, Spanish-Pueblo Revival and Territorial. Before the railroad arrived in 1880, Santa Fe had been forced by necessity to build from mud bricks and unmilled tree trunks. No one thought it was attractive or special or tourism-worthy. There were a few Territorial buildings prior to 1880 with bricks and millwork produced locally, but only a few.

The railroad brought tools, Victorian and Greek Revival architecture, brick, glass, and milled lumber. Santa Fe quickly started to look like the rest of America. From the arrival of the railroad in 1880 to about 1920, Santa Fe was building brick houses with peaked roofs. Many are still standing, stucco-free, along East Palace and in the South Capitol district.

Beginning in about 1912, there was talk of returning Santa Fe to its pre-railroad appearance. The city started to encourage building in "New-Old Santa Fe Style," which meant the rounded, adobe look of Spanish-Pueblo Revival. The style melded elements of the local Indian pueblos with the structures of Spanish settlers. The definitive history of exactly how and why this occurred, and who the principal movers were, is given in Chris Wilson's *The Myth of Santa Fe*. By 1913 Santa Fe's anticipated architectural transformation was described in the local newspaper, *The New Mexican*.

When did the first Spanish-Pueblo Revival appear in Santa Fe? Taos Pueblo had been known for centuries but no one imitated it until about 1911 - 13. That was the period of the drastic remodeling of the Palace of the Governors, led by Jesse Nusbaum, into its present appearance, with rounded edges and protruding exterior *vigas*. The building had served as the capitol until 1883. From 1894 to 1909 it served as the Territorial Law Library, the home of Territorial Governor L. Bradford Prince, and display rooms for the Historical Society of New Mexico. Then in 1909 it became the Museum of New Mexico.

The next major step was the 1915 Panama-California Exposition in San Diego, where many states were represented with localized architecture. The New Mexico Building designed by Rapp & Rapp was a hit. Its principal inspiration was the Spanish Mission churches at Acoma, Laguna, and San Felipe pueblos. Spanish-Pueblo Revival became the definitive future of Santa Fe. Immediately after the San Diego exposition, people started remodeling and building on the Santa Fe Plaza. Major buildings that got the ball rolling were the

Fine Arts Museum in 1917, the Gross Kelly Warehouse in 1920, La Fonda hotel in 1922, the Carlos Vierra house built between 1918 and 1922, and the post office on Cathedral Place (now the Institute of American Indian Arts) in 1921.

Who first inspired Santa Fe's architectural style? The style's inspiration may have been Adolf Bandelier, a Swiss-American explorer who lived on East DeVargas Street in Santa Fe from 1880 to 1882. He surveyed Pueblo Indian sites, including Pecos and Cochiti pueblos and Frijoles Canyon, 20 miles north of Santa Fe, now named Bandelier National Monument. But he had no role in replicating the style in Santa Fe.

Shortly after Bandolier departed, archeologist Edgar Lee Hewett (1865 - 1946) arrived and founded the School of American Archeology in 1907 (now known as the School of Advanced Research) and the Museum of New Mexico in 1909. For 30 years, Hewett lived at 116 Grant, originally a

Fort Marcy officers' quarters. Hewett played a major role in developing interest in indigenous cultures of the southwest. Under Hewett's direction, many young archeologists came to New Mexico to work at Frijoles Canyon and other ruins.

The first architects to build in Spanish-Pueblo Revival were Isaac and William Rapp of the firm Rapp & Rapp, based in Trinidad, Colorado. The Rapps designed the Gross Kelly Warehouse (1913), the Fine Arts Museum (1917), and the original La Fonda Hotel (1922).

William Penhallow Henderson, an artist and architect who lived in Santa Fe from 1916 to 1943, was an influential proponent of Spanish-Pueblo Revival. He and his son-in-law, John Evans, founded a design firm called the Pueblo-Spanish Building Company.

Architect John Gaw Meem (1894 - 1983) arrived in Santa Fe in 1920, about eight years after Spanish-Pueblo Revival had taken hold. However, Meem was instrumental in establishing it as New Mexico's predominant architecture. Meem did not invent the style but he was its champion. He headed the committee that authored the 1957 Historical Zoning Ordinance, which required all future buildings in central Santa Fe to adhere to either Spanish-Pueblo Revival or Territorial Revival style. Many of his buildings were private homes.

In Santa Fe Meem's public buildings include the Laboratory of Anthropology (1931), the 1927 expansion of La Fonda Hotel, First Presbyterian Church (1937), Christo Rey Church (1939), and the County Courthouse (1938). In Albuquerque, his buildings include UNM's Zimmerman Library (1938), Scholes Hall (1934), Los Poblanos Historic Inn (1936) and the Student Union, now called the Anthropology Building (1936). His principal works were completed between 1929 and 1960. His home was at 785 Camino del Monte Sol.

Visitors often inquire about the distinction between "real abobe" and "fake adobe." Real adobe means the walls are made from mud and straw bricks, without a steel frame. Most of Santa Fe's historic buildings are fake adobe, including the Fine Arts Museum, Gross Kelly Warehouse, Christo Rey Church, and La Fonda. Real adobe is used in private homes, not in commercial, government, or church buildings.

A search of the archives of *The New York Times* reveals that Santa Fe's focus on tourism, its effort to preserve its history, buildings, traditions, and its resistance to modernization, go back a long way. On May 19, 1929, it published an article titled "Santa Fe, Aloof, Clings to its Heritage. The Famous Old Trail City is Making a Determined Stand to Keep its Vivid Life from Booms and Skyscrapers." *The New York Times* reported on Santa Fe's battle to preserve itself in the 1940s, 1950s, 1960s, and 1970s. Beginning in 1947, it also published every decade or so, a sightseeing guide to Santa Fe.

The Old Santa Fe Association was founded in 1926 to encourage historic preservation laws. Its preservation and restoration arm, the Historic Santa Fe Foundation, was founded in 1961 and published its first historic tour map in 1962. Today the organization's website lists more than 70 structures that it deems "worthy of preservation."

Reverse direction, walk back on Galisteo, then right on Water

The Greyhound bus station used to be on Water between Galisteo and Don Gaspar, in the building that is now Coyote Café. It was a cosmopolitan place with character bestowed by travelers. It moved to St. Michaels Drive in 1985. The new bus station is a generic, lonely eyesore with plastic seats and no character. (See photo on page 74.)

The building at the corner of 120 Don Gaspar, at the corner with Water St., was built in 1870 as a hotel called the Normandie, later the National, and in its last years, the Montezuma. The retail shop called Doodlet's has been open since 1955. It closed for 18 months in 2006 - 07 while the building was renovated by its owner, Theo Raven. Three condominiums were added to the building.

Café Pasqual, opened by chef/owner Katharine Kagel in 1979, is across from Doodlet's. The history of the building and Pasqual's is told on www.chefjohnnyvee.com. An excerpt from the website states:

> *The building, at the corner of Don Gaspar and Water Street plays a rich part in Santa Fe history. Originally a Texaco gas station, it first became a food establishment in 1923 as The Liberty Café. In 1935 it became the K.C. Waffle House, famous for their Kansas City Steaks and location across from the bus station housed in the building that would become The Coyote Café. The Waffle House was open 24 hours and welcomed weary bus travels to the remote western town, at any hour. Perhaps to remind Kagel of her roots, the original neon sign from K.C.'s sits in her back yard. The neon tubes have long been broken, but Kagel would love to stir the memory of a longtime Santa*

Fean and find out the exact colors of the gas that illuminated the sign and rebuild and relight it.

> *In 1954, it was transformed it into The Mayflower Café, which had been located on the south side of the Plaza from 1936 to 1954. The Mayflower enjoyed a 16-year life there until it became The Golden Temple of Conscious Cookery in 1970. Run by the Sikh community the healthy food of the Temple gave way to Pogo's, a submarine sandwich shop, in 1977, perhaps a sign of the changing times.*

The fountain at the corner of Water and Don Gaspar was installed in 1987 by stonemason Thomas Lipps. It was one of the first city-funded public art projects. It flowed during warm weather until 2002, when the region experienced a drought and water-use restrictions resulted in shutting the fountain off.

The Hotel St. Francis on Don Gaspar was previously a hotel called the De Vargas Hotel. The first De Vargas Hotel, a wood Victorian at the corner of Washington and Marcy, burned to the ground in January 1922. It was replaced by the new The De Vargas Hotel, which opened on Don Gaspar in 1924 as the city's finest hotel. "It was a first-class hotel where men wore top hats and ladies wore full-length dresses and bellhops escorted the guests to their rooms."[2] It remained the city's best hotel until the 1940s, when new hotels started opening. The De Vargas became seedy and gradually ran down until it was finally closed in 1983. Under new ownership, the hotel was renovated and reopened in 1986 as the upscale St. Francis. In 2009 the new owners of the St. Francis, Heritage Hotels and Resorts, proceeded to tear out the hotel's historic and stately lobby and replace it with an artificial theme lobby that the new owners describe as "a historical appearance reflecting the simple and spiritual style of the Franciscan Missionary Order."

Steaksmith restaurant was located on the De Vargas Hotel's ground floor in leased space from the time of the restaurant's opening in 1973 until the hotel's new owners arrived in 1983. At that time Steaksmith moved to its current location next door to El Gancho on Old Las Vegas Highway.

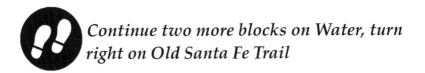

Continue two more blocks on Water, turn right on Old Santa Fe Trail

At the northwest corner of Water and Old Santa Fe Trail, there is an undeveloped corner site with outdoor carts selling tourist items. In the 1960s and '70s this was a gas station known as Le Bow's Chevron Station.

Next to corner site is 125 E. Water Street, the location of Catamount Bar and Grille for the 15 years from 1995 to 2010. Prior to The Catamount this site was the original location of The Candyman Music Store.

Turn right on Old Santa Fe Trail. Loretto Chapel was built from 1873 to 1878 as a school chapel. The Gothic Revival design copies the famous and much larger Sainte-Chapelle in Paris. Sandstone to build the chapel was quarried near Lamy and the ornate stained glass windows were made in Paris. After Loretto Academy closed in 1968, its chapel was deconsecrated as a Catholic church. It is now owned by a private owner, not the hotel, and is open to the public for a fee, and available for weddings and even for church services offered by an independent church.

Loretto Academy of Our Lady of Light, a Catholic school for girls, was located on the site that is now the Inn at Loretto. The school was founded in 1853 by four nuns, the Sisters of Loretto, under the direction of Bishop Jean-Baptiste Lamy. Many generations of girls in Santa Fe were educated at the school in grades 1 through 12. The school was surrounded on three sides by a red brick wall and on the fourth side, facing Old Santa Fe Trail, by a wrought-iron fence. There were five principal buildings: Loretto chapel, a four-story classroom building, a residential building where the boarders and nuns lived, an administration building, and an auditorium.[3]

When Loretto closed in 1968, its assets were transferred to St. Michael's High School, which became co-ed at that date. Except the chapel, all the school buildings were razed in the early 1970s. The Inn at Loretto, a hotel designed to look like Taos Pueblo, opened on the site in 1975, preserving the name Loretto.

CIVILIAN CONSERVATION CORPS

From 1933 to 1942, the Civilian Conservation Corps, a New Deal program, was active in New Mexico. It built roads, parks, dams, buildings, and schools. The CCC shut down in 1942 because its workers were needed by the military in World War II.

In 1938 it built Hyde Park Lodge, with its thick stone walls and massive roof of timbers. It also built Hyde Park Road as far as Aspen Vista and Santa Fe's first rope tow for skiing, in Hyde Park, just above the lodge.

Hyde Park Road was not extended to the ski mountain until around 1948. That was when Chuck LeFever built three rope tows at the ski mountain. Two or three years later, the Bohlander family installed the first chair lift using old mining equipment. In February 1950 Santa Fe Ski Basin opened for skiing with one chairlift. In its initial years, it was managed by Ernie Blake, who had been hired by Santa Fe Ski Corp. Blake moved to Taos in 1955 to found Taos Ski Valley. The first ski lift in Taos was built in 1956.

In 1937 - 39 the CCC built the Old Santa Fe Trail Building to serve as the National Park Service regional office. The building is a sterling example of Spanish-Pueblo Revival architecture with walls two to five feet thick. The CCC also built the road to Bandolier National Monument and 31 Spanish-Pueblo Revival buildings around Frijoles Canyon. In 1934 the CCC built the Don Gaspar bridge over the Santa Fe River.

In 2009 a statue to honor the CCC was dedicated near the sidewalk of Don Gaspar on the west side of the Capitol.

Reverse direction, walk east on Water to St. Francis Cathedral

St. Francis Cathedral was built between 1869 and 1886 under the direction of Bishop Jean-Baptiste Lamy. It is in the Romanesque Revival style, and its specific inspiration was the medieval churches of Clermont-Ferrand, France. The ground under the Cathedral is five feet higher than the area around it. That ground is the rubble of the first four churches on that site.

The first church on the site was built shortly after the city's founding in 1608 and lasted until 1630. The second church was built in 1631 and remained until it was destroyed in the Pueblo Revolt of 1680. The Spanish returned to Santa Fe in 1692 but did not built a new church until 1714. This third church, called La Parroquia, lasted until 1869. It was rebuilt in the early 1800s, which some historians consider to be a fourth church on the site. When St. Francis Cathedral was built, the giant alter from La Parroquia was saved and is now used at Christo Rey Church. Bishop Lamy arrived in Santa Fe in 1851 and remained until his death in 1888.

Over its 17 years of construction, there was a line of architects and masons from France and Italy who came to Santa Fe specifically to work on the Cathedral. In 2008 - 09, it was entirely shrouded in tarpaulins while it received a through interior and exterior facelift. In front of the Cathedral there are statues of Saint Francis and Archbishop J.B. Lamy.

Across from St. Francis Cathedral is The Institute of American Indian Arts Museum. Originally this was the known to locals as "the federal building." It was built in 1921 to house the U.S. Post Office and other federal offices. Note the cornerstone at the northeast corner. It was among the first buildings constructed in Spanish-Pueblo Revival style. It was sold to Institute of American Indian Arts (IAIA) after construction of the Montoya Federal Building on Federal Place in 1963.

On Palace Ave. is the historic La Casa Sena. It was built in stages as a private residence until it reached a total of 33 rooms. The largest business inside, a restaurant called La Casa Sena, opened in 1983. The interior courtyard is wonderfully preserved. Note the cabinet next to Goler shoes containing historic artifacts and a timeline of the building's history. The Shed restaurant opened on Burro Alley in 1953 in a shed formerly used to house burros, and later moved to La Casa Sena.

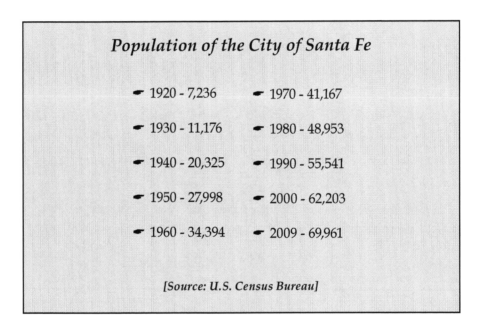

Population of the City of Santa Fe

- 1920 - 7,236
- 1930 - 11,176
- 1940 - 20,325
- 1950 - 27,998
- 1960 - 34,394
- 1970 - 41,167
- 1980 - 48,953
- 1990 - 55,541
- 2000 - 62,203
- 2009 - 69,961

[Source: U.S. Census Bureau]

Walk to Washington and turn right

The Burrito Company at 111 Washington opened in 1984. Previously the location was Washington Street Deli, which closed in 1983. The Territorial-style building dates to the 1860s and has been modified many times.

Construction of the Inn of The Anasazi, a Pueblo-style hotel, was completed in 1991. Previously that site was occupied by the State Securities Building, which housed the state correctional department and the juvenile jail.

Across from Inn of The Anasazi is the back door of The New Mexico History Museum. This 96,000 square foot building opened in May 2009 after three years of construction in the narrow space behind Palace of the Governors.

Look at the Territorial-style building that reads "Public Library" in large letters around the front door. The building was built in 1907 as the Woman's Board of Trade Building. In 1932 - 34 John Gaw Meem transformed its brick exterior into Santa Fe style and it became the public library. It was renovated again in 1963. When the library moved out in 1988, the building was acquired by the Museum of New Mexico to become the Museum of New Mexico's archives, officially the "History Library and Photo Annex." It was renovated for the third time in 1996. When it was the library, it had a portal, big windows, and graceful pillars. In 1989 - 90 the History Museum tore off the front of the building and made it a solid wall, thus erasing its history. The building has four cornerstones: 1907, 1932, 1963, and 1996.

Now look at the Hotel Chimayo, which was built in 1990, on the corner of Washington and Nusbaum. This was the location of the graceful, magnificent Civil War era, two-story, territorial-style Simon Nusbaum house. In 1961, despite protests, the city demolished The Nusbaum house. It was built by Jewish pioneer merchant Solomon Spiegelberg and was later owned by Simon Nusbaum, a key figure in Santa Fe in the early 20th century who photographed the city extensively in that era. For 29 years, from 1961 to 1990, the city used the site as an 85-car parking lot. In 1990 the site was sold and Hotel Chimayo was built. The senseless destruction of the Nusbaum house by the city council sparked efforts to amend the 1957 ordinance to protect historic buildings, and it also led to the creation of the Historic Santa Fe Foundation.

In 1988 the library moved into its present location. This building was constructed in 1937 to serve as a municipal building containing city hall, the municipal court, the police station, and a few jail cells. In 1986 - 88 the building was renovated to become the main library and the police and city hall moved to their present locations.

First Interstate Plaza, a pair of four-story office buildings at 150 Washington, occupies most of the block between Washington, Lincoln, and Marcy. It was proposed in 1980 and built in 1982 - 1983. There was great opposition to this building, which replaced single-story shops and the historic Governor Miguel Otero residence. The approval by Historic Design Review Committee was opposed by many preservationists and the project was widely disliked by residents of Santa Fe.

DOWNTOWN'S FILLING STATIONS

In the 1950s and '60s, downtown Santa Fe contained an astonishing number of gas stations, which were known as "filling stations" in those days. Filling stations were much smaller than today's service stations and often were placed on corners. Flipping through old phone directories shows that many downtown filling stations had short lives, and they frequently changed names. Based on the memories of today's old-timers, about 10 of those filling stations were firmly established and known to everyone in town, usually by the name of the proprietor.

- The last remaining filling station from those days was the Old Trail Garage on Old Santa Fe Trail, which opened in 1948 and closed in 2009. It had been a Texaco but changed to an independent in its last few years. The property owner was unable to sell the lot due to its zoning in the Business Capitol district, which restricts usage. So in 2010 it was returned to its prior use as an automotive repair shop, without the gasoline pumps.

- The bank at the northeast corner of Washington and Marcy was a filling station called Benny's Gulf Station, then later Rudy's Exxon, until 1994. In that year the Historic Design Review Board approved remodeling the building for a bank. The old tin ceiling is still in place above the ATM machine, which sits where the gas pumps were.

- As late as 1983 the parking lot on Washington Ave. adjacent to Osteria d'Assisi restaurant was Charlie Davis's Service Station, known in its later years as Courtesy Exxon.

- The corner of West Palace and Grant, which is now galleries and an upstairs restaurant, was a filling station known by the name if its owner, Cecil Sherwood's Chevron Station. It closed in 1982. The filling station first opened in 1929, became Sherwood's in 1945, and remained Sherwood's until it closed.

- The northwest corner of Water St. and Old Santa Fe Trail, now an outdoor market for tourist goods, was a filling station known as Le Bow's Chevron Station.

- The corner of East Alameda and Old Santa Fe Trail, which is now Mangiamo Pronto and some tourist shops, was Kenny Moore's filling station.

- The location of Del Charro restaurant, at the corner of Don Gaspar and West Alameda Street, was a filling station.

- The corner of Galisteo and West Alameda, which had been Evangelo's Mediterranean Café and became Tomme Restaurant in 2011, was a filling station.

- The northeast corner of the Plaza, which today is Frank Howell Gallery, was Vic's Conoco station until 1976.

☞ The southeast corner of Galisteo and Water Streets, by the former bus station, was Paul Ragle's filling station. It is now a small furniture store called Sequoia. Ragle Park on Rodeo Road is named after Paul Ragle.

 *Turn right on Marcy and walk one block*

The north side of the block of Marcy between Washington and Otero Street is today mostly occupied by an office building, Marcy Plaza. From 1881 to 1922, this block was occupied by Santa Fe's grandest hotel, a large wooden Victorian named the Palace Hotel until 1910 when its name was changed to the De Vargas Hotel. It was built to provide a luxury hotel for people arriving on the newly built railroad. It burned to the ground in 1922, with newspaper headline describing it as the "Biggest fire in the history of city." The block was left vacant until 1931, when houses were built, much like the brick bungalows on the next block to the east. In 1981 the block of houses was razed to allow construction of Marcy Plaza in 1982 - 83.

Across from Marcy Plaza offices, at 120 E. Marcy, there is a one-story commercial building called The Healy Building. The Video Library operated from the corner location for 21 years, from 1988 until 2010, when it moved to the Harvey Building on Paseo de Peralta. It originally opened in 1981 in Crossroads Center, at the corner of Cerrillos and St. Francis.

For a short period prior to The Video Library, in the mid-1980s, the space at 120 was a computer store, and prior to that it was Paris Shoes.

Walk back to the corner of Marcy and Washington, and look right up Washington. On the northeast corner is US Bank. This was a filling station called Benny's Gulf, and later Rudy's Exxon, until 1994. Note the original tin ceiling above the ATM machine, where the gas pumps stood. (See photo on page 76.)

Immediately to the north of Benny's Gulf Station was Dee's Restaurant, which was open from 1976 to 1997, and was known for its donuts and green chile cheeseburgers. Today the former Dee's is El Mesón Restaurant. North of El Mesón is the Padre Gallegos House, built 1857 - 1862 by Padre Gallegos, a colorful priest and politician of that era. He was the last of the Spanish Catholic priests to lead Santa Fe's parish. In 1852 he was defrocked by the stern Bishop Lamy, who arrived in Santa Fe from France in 1851. Today the Padre Gallegos House is home to Santa Café restaurant and Sotheby's.

Directly across from US Bank is Washington Federal Bank. This was Kaune's Grocery Co. from 1956 to May 2001. When it closed, the store's long-time manager and part-owner was Hank Wells. He was the great-grandson of Harry S. Kaune, who first opened Kaune's Grocery Co. in 1896. Wells attributed the store's closing to the opening of Whole Foods, which opened in 2000. When Kaune's closed the building was in poor condition. Charter Bank gutted and renovated the entire structure and restored the exterior corbels and woodwork. In 2011 Charter Bank was replaced by Washington Federal Bank.

Key Architectural Terms

Spanish Colonial: buildings close to the street edge, zaguans, inner courtyards called placitas, portales along the street and the interior courtyards, lintals.

Spanish-Pueblo Revival: a flat roof with parapet and canales, uneven walls, deeply recessed windows, portals, projecting vigas on the exterior, exposed vigas and latillas on the interiors. It can be real adobe (sun-dried mud and straw bricks) or fake adobe.

Territorial: Territorial has flat roofs and brown stucco walls. It is modified from Pueblo-style with brick coping, white-painted, milled woodwork windows, and square portal posts. Territorial-style buildings are often two-story.

Human scale: Buildings, structures, and signs are not much bigger than humans. In contrast with other cities, things are shorter and smaller.

Continue west on Marcy, then left on Lincoln toward the Plaza

La Esquina Building, a five-story building at the corner of Lincoln and Marcy, was built in 1980 - 82 as an office building. The building deteriorated rapidly and in 2008, after only 26 years, it was stripped to the steel beams and rebuilt as retail and condominiums for office and residential occupants.

Prior to 1980, the site was occupied by a Queen Anne-style house, set back about 50 feet from Marcy Street and facing Lincoln Ave. In that 50-foot strip between the side of the house and Marcy Street, someone, probably in the 1940s, built a one-story commercial building. For decades that building was home to two businesses. There was the Little Chief Grill, a simple restaurant popular with high school students who attend Santa Fe High, which was across the street. And there was Durr's Office Machines, a typewriter store owned by Harold Durr. The Queen Anne-style house, Little Chief Grill, and Durr's were razed in the late 1970s to clear the land for La Esquina. During construction of La Esquina, graffiti on the plywood surrounding the project read "Coming soon! 5-story fake adobe skyscraper courtesy of City Hall."

Sears Roebuck was just off the Plaza at 130 Lincoln. In 1990 it moved to Villa Linda Mall on the south side of town. In 1991 the old Sears building on Lincoln was renovated, divided to provide space for shops and offices, and dubbed Lincoln Place.

Next door to Sears was Cartwright's Plumbing, a downtown presence from 1939 until it moved to Osage Avenue in 1973. It started as Broome Hardware, located at 127 West San Francisco St. In 1939 it was purchased by Bill Cartwright and changed its name to Cartwright's Plumbing. In 1949 Cartwright's acquired a competitor, Wood-Davis Hardware, which was located at 120 Lincoln Ave, and moved to that location, which was next to Sears.

Across the street from Sears were a grocery called Batrite's and an appliance store called The Maytag Shop. Those buildings were demolished in 1980 to clear the site for the First Interstate Building.

On the corner of Lincoln and Palace, which is the northwest corner of the Plaza, sits the New Mexico Museum of Arts, formerly the Fine Arts Museum. When it was built in 1917, it was a startling and bold effort to push Santa Fe in the direction of Spanish-Pueblo Revival.

Los Alamos

Santa Fe remained an obscure place until World War II. In 1942 the federal government was searching for a location to develop the atomic bomb. The chief physicist on the Manhattan Project was Robert Oppenheimer, who had attended Los Alamos Ranch School as a boy. On his recommendation, Los Alamos was selected, both for its remoteness and its beauty. In early 1943 the Army took over the Los Alamos Ranch School. Los Alamos changed Santa Fe drastically. It brought airmail (replaced surface mail), federal jobs, business contracts with the lab, new visitors and residents, roads, educated people, traffic, and commercial flights to Santa Fe Airport.

Turn around, walk north on Lincoln to South Federal Place

At 207 Lincoln, between Century Bank and an office building, there is a parking lot suitable for approximately 30 cars. There was a commercial building on that site from 1954 to 1985. It was built in a style called California Stick Modern Chalet, and thus did not respect Spanish-Pueblo Revival style. The building served until 1978 as an architecture office and interior design shop. From 1979 to 1985 it served as a hot tub business called The Soak Hot Tub Club. The Soak closed in 1985 and the building was razed.

Construction on the U.S. Federal Courthouse on Federal Place began in 1853. It is Santa Fe's sole remaining Greek Revival architecture. Originally it was planned to serve as the territorial capitol. Lincoln Ave. was laid in 1866 and designed to run from the Plaza to the capitol. However the building took 36 years to complete, principally because of funding delays, and at completion in 1889, it was redesignated to serve as federal offices. The Kit Carson Memorial, which stands in front of the building, was placed in 1885, four years prior to the building's completion. The stone obelisk was funded and cut by Stephen W. Dorsey, a wealthy Vermont-born civil war veteran who lived in New Mexico in the 1880s. The building's north side was an addition in 1929 - 30. The Federal Courthouse is open to the public and worth seeing inside for its six murals by William P. Henderson.

The stone wall surrounding the building is called the Federal Oval. In 1883 a racetrack was built for horses and burro races. The stone wall was the inside rail of the racetrack, though it has probably not been used for races since those days.

Century Bank, which faces the Federal Courthouse, first opened in Santa Fe in 1887 and remains locally owned. The building was constructed in 1970, when the bank was still known as Mutual Building & Loan Association.

To the north of the Federal Courthouse, across Paseo de Peralta (formerly North Federal Place), is the Scottish Rite Temple. This is a Masonic Lodge, completed in 1912 in Moorish Revival style. Its appearance is based on the Alhambra in Seville, Spain. Inside it contains a 300-seat theater and a 400-seat ballroom. The Temple is open to the public for tours Monday through Friday, 9am to noon and 1 to 4 p.m.

The property to the west of the Masonic Lodge has long been owned by the Presbyterian Church. From 1866 to 1959, this was the site of the Allison-James School, a Presbyterian school.[4]

Walk back to Marcy Street, turn right at City Hall

Today's City Hall building was constructed in 1951 - 53 as Santa Fe High School, and served that role until 1972. The new high school was built on Siringo Road in 1972, and grades 10 - 12 moved into that building. At that time, the old high school building on Marcy Street was renamed Santa Fe Mid-High School and used only to serve grade 9. Its role as Santa Fe Mid-High lasted only three years, with the last class graduating in 1975. In 1976 the building was acquired by the City. After renovation it was dedicated as City Hall in 1977.

The first public school in Santa Fe, called the Catron School and serving grades 1 through 12, was built on the site that became Santa Fe High School. Designed by architect I.H. Rapp, it was a beautiful four-story brick building with a peaked roof. The Catron School was built in 1904 and razed in 1951 to allow for construction of the nondescript new high school. The headline in *The New Mexican* on November 29, 1950 stated "Landmark goes, Old Catron Building Bows to Modernity."

The Convention Center opened in September 2008. It occupies the site of the former Sweeney Gymnasium, which was the high school gym from 1955 to 1975. Then the school district sold it (along with the classroom building next door) to the city, and the building was modified to serve as Sweeney Convention Center which opened in 1979 and was razed in 2006.

Prior to construction of Sweeney Gym in 1955, there was an old high school classroom building called the Sena Building on the site. The Sena Building had been built in the 19th century as the hospital for Fort Marcy. It became the high school in 1900 and was demolished in 1954 to clear space for Sweeney Gymnasium.

The office across Marcy from the Convention Center was originally part of Santa Fe High School. The building was known as the Band Building because the school band practiced there. The building was also used for shop classes. The building has been well-maintained and today contains law offices.

When you reach Grant you are looking at the side of First Presbyterian Church. In 1867 First Presbyterian Church was established and a year later, in 1868, it purchased the ruins of an adobe church at the corner of Grant and Marcy. The church remains at that location. The present church building was designed by John Gaw Meem, constructed in 1939, and renovated and expanded in 2005.

Behind First Presbyterian Church is the First Judicial District courthouse. The building was originally a junior high school, Leah Harvey Junior High, which was built in 1937 and closed in 1976. The building was renovated and opened for business as a courthouse in 1978.

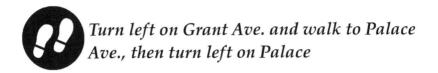 Turn left on Grant Ave. and walk to Palace Ave., then turn left on Palace

The front entrance of First Presbyterian Church is where Griffin St. and Grant Ave. intersect. There is a historic house at 136 Griffin Street known as the Tully House, which now serves as a classic example of Territorial architecture. This 1851 adobe was built by Pinckney Randolph Tully, a trader and merchant who has now been largely forgotten by history, except for his house.

Turn left and walk down Grant Ave. The building occupied by Riva Yares Gallery on Grant Ave. was a Safeway grocery store for 43 years, from 1942 to 1985.

The vacant building at 142 West Palace was the Palace Restaurant from 1961 to 2005. Its glory days of the 1960s, '70s, and '80s were past. For 20 years, from 1983 to 2003, it was owned by Lino Pertusini, who sold it in 2003. He remains the owner of Osteria d'Assisi, a restaurant on Federal Place. The new owner of The Palace tried to re-energize the restaurant but failed, and it was sold to new owners in 2005. The new owners re-opened it as a new restaurant called Senior Lucky's, which lasted less than two years and closed in 2007. It was vacant from 2007 to 2011, then re-opened as a new restaurant that preserves the name Palace Restaurant as well as the saloon style and dark red velvet wallpaper for which the old Palace Restaurant was famous.

Until 1961, Frank's Cocktail Lounge occupied the site that became the Palace Restaurant. In 1961 Frank's moved 530 Cerrillos Road, on the site now occupied by the Hotel Santa Fe, and remained there until it closed in 1979.

In the 1800s, the site of the Palace Restaurant site was a legendary saloon and bordello that catered to cowboys and fur trappers. In 1837 a Mexican woman known as Doña Tules established an infamous and elaborate gambling establishment on the site. She was a colorful figure in that period of the city's history and her biography, *Doña Tules: Santa Fe's Courtesan and Gambler*, captures the story.

Santa Fe's daily newspaper, *The New Mexican*, has been published without interruption since 1849. Prior to World War II it was located at 123 West Palace, a two-story building at the corner of West Palace Street and Sheridan Avenue, which today contains an art gallery. In the 1940s *The New Mexican* constructed a new building for itself at 202 East Marcy, and has remained at that site ever since, though the building itself was gutted and rebuilt in 2007.

At 124 W. Palace is the historic Felipe B. Delgado house, built in 1891 and a good example of Territorial architecture.

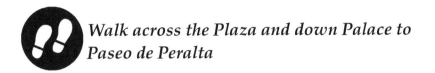

Walk across the Plaza and down Palace to Paseo de Peralta

In 1865, nuns from Sisters of Charity arrived from Ohio and opened a small adobe hospital, an orphanage, and the St. Vincent Tuberculosis Sanatorium (the spelling the Sisters of Charity used, to designate the treatment of tuberculosis rather than the less-specific "sanitarium"). The location was behind St. Francis Cathedral, on the land now occupied by old St. Vincent Hospital, Marion Hall, and their parking lot. The sanatorium was destroyed by fire in 1896. The site was vacant until 1911 when a new St. Vincent Sanatorium was constructed. In 1953, when the new St. Vincent hospital opened, the sanatorium ceased operating, the building was renamed Marian Hall, and it became a convent (the first two floors) and a residence for nurses (third floor).

In January 1953 St. Vincent Hospital opened two new hospital buildings at the corner of Palace and Paseo de Peralta (which was then a smaller street called Castillo). There was the main hospital building and the attached La Villa Rivera building. Both buildings were designed by John Gaw Meem. From 1953 to 1977 St. Vincent Hospital operated in those two buildings, before moving to its new building on St. Michael's drive in 1977.

In 1978 the state of New Mexico purchased the old St. Vincent hospital to use as state offices. In 2003 the state sold the five-acre site to private investors, who made no changes in the buildings. In 2007 the private investors sold the property to Drury Hotels for $20 million. Drury plans to build two hotels, a 181-room Drury hotel in the old St. Vincent building and a 30-room boutique hotel in Marian Hall. The southern portion of the site, where the former St. Francis Cathedral School and a parking lot are located, is owned by the Archdiocese. In 2010 the New

Mexico School for the Arts, a new charter school, leased the former St. Francis Cathedral School.

Across the street from old St. Vincent Hospital at 237 West Palace is the Spiegelberg House, now occupied by Peyton-Wright Gallery. The gallery's website states:

> *Peyton Wright Gallery is located at 237 East Palace Avenue in the meticulously preserved Spiegelberg house. The house was built in 1880 by Willie Spiegelberg, one of five brothers who moved to Santa Fe in the mid 19th century to form the influential Spiegelberg Brothers' mercantile firm. The Willie Spiegelberg House was designed by a French architect who utilized European artisans and craftsmen. The house is of adobe construction with many fine European architectural details. Territorial design is evident in both the exterior and interior of the building. Solomon Spitz, founder of the S. Spitz Jewelry and Manufacturing Company in Santa Fe, bought the house in 1900 and lived there until 1963 when it was sold to Dr. Edward Cook, a local dentist and former chairman of the Historic Santa Fe Foundation Board of Directors. In 1973 the building was listed with the National Register of Historic Places. John Wright Schaefer, the current Proprietor and owner of Peyton Wright Gallery, restored much of the building to its original state for the gallery's inaugural exhibition on May 1, 1998.*

WHEN WAS PASEO DE PERALTA BUILT?

Paseo de Peralta was constructed in 1972 - 1974 by linking and widening several smaller streets that formed a nearly complete loop around downtown. The catalyst for this project was De-Vargas Center, which opened in 1973.

The north portion was created from a road called North Federal Place, which until 1972, stopped at Grant Street. In 1972 North Federal Place was extended to intersect Guadalupe (then still called Rosario Street) and renamed Paseo de Peralta.

The east and south portions were created in 1973 - 1974 from Hillside, Castillo, Hickox, and Manhattan Streets. Castillo Street ran from Canyon Road to Marcy Street. It no longer exists but a reminder is extant in the form of a tiny, one-block street off the former Castillo Street called Castillo Place. Hillside was a narrow dirt road running from Marcy Street around the curve to Washington Ave. Manhattan and Hickox were longer than their current length. Hickox merged into Manhattan Street just before the Roundhouse, and Manhattan extended to Acequia Madre Street. Manhattan and Castillo Streets did not intersect. Several tiny one-block streets that no longer exist were at that location.

OLD SANTA FE IN PICTURES

San Francisco Street at Plaza, 1961. Photographer unknown, Courtesy Palace of the Governors Photo Archives, (NMHM/DCA), negative 051359

San Francisco Street at Plaza, 1947. Martin, Robert H. Courtesy Palace of the Governors Photo Archives, (NMHM/DCA), negative 030927

East San Francisco Street at Plaza, 1940 - 43? Frasher, Courtesy Palace of the Governors Photo Archives, (NMHM/DCA), negative 106739

East San Francisco Street at Plaza, 1955, Buell, C., Courtesy Palace of the Governors Photo Archives, (NMHM/DCA), negative 091542

The Streets of Santa Fe

East San Francisco Street at Plaza, date unknown, photographer unknown, Courtesy Palace of the Governors Photo Archives, (NMHM/DCA), negative 177284

Boy Scouts on the Plaza, date unknown, photographer unknown, Courtesy Palace of the Governors Photo Archives, (NMHM/DCA), negative 011356

El Paseo Theater, 1959. Dingee, Tyler. Courtesy Palace of the Governors Photo Archives, (NMHM/DCA), negative 091900

Union Bus Depot, 1925 - 1945? Parkhurst, T. Harmon. Courtesy Palace of the Governors Photo Archives, (NMHM/DCA), negative 051111

San Francisco Street, 1911 - 12. Parkhurst, T. Harmon, Courtesy Palace of the Governors Photo Archives, (NMHM/DCA), negative 012158

Gulf Service Station, 1983 - 84, Washington Ave. at Marcy St. Wilder, Richard. Courtesy Palace of the Governors Photo Archives, (NMHM/DCA), negative 147973

CANYON ROAD

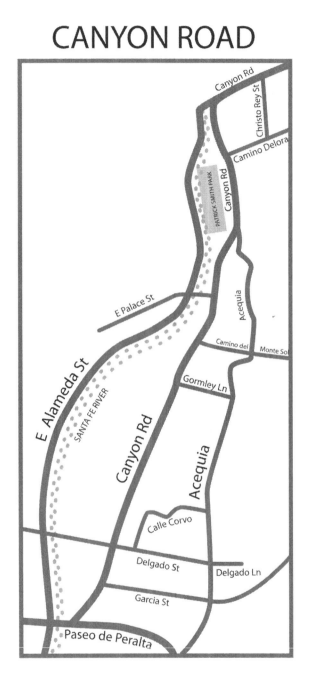

Turn right on Paseo de Peralta, walk to Canyon Road, walk up Canyon Road

It's best to walk Canyon Road on a Saturday or Sunday morning, when you can have it to yourself, without the cars. It's exactly one mile to Christo Rey Church, and everyone should walk this entire length. The upper half of Canyon Road, another mile beyond the church, is residential and not essential.

Until 1964 Canyon Road was unpaved and residential. There were farm animals and orchards of fruit trees behind the homes. The road was hard packed dirt, or impassable mud in the rainy summers. In the 1910s, artists started moving to Santa Fe, making Santa Fe an art colony. In the early 1960s Canyon Road had a coffeehouse called Three Cities of Spain and three grocery stores but no art galleries. The groceries were Percy's, Gormley's, and Friendly's.

The walk begins at the bottom of Canyon Road. An early group of galleries opened in 1971 at the compound that become known as The Streets of Taos, at the southeast corner of Canyon Road and Paseo de Peralta. It was run by Harold and Hilda Street, flamboyant art dealers from Taos who drove his and her Rolls Royces. The Streets of Taos Compound includes three addresses that compose most of the triangular block formed by East DeVargas St., Paseo de Peralta, and Canyon Road.

The brick building that houses Ventana Fine Art, at the corner of Garcia Street, was the First Ward School, a schoolhouse constructed in 1906. Santa Fe in those days was divided into wards. The First Ward School was built by Italian stonemason Carlo Digneo, who came to Santa Fe in 1880 to work on St. Francis Cathedral. He built a number of other prominent brick homes in Santa Fe such as 1231 Paseo de Peralta.

After the First Ward School is a low building with a front yard at 414 Canyon. This house was built in 1730s and may be the oldest building on Canyon Road.

553 Canyon is the Edwin Brooks house, which was the last home of artist Fremont Ellis, who lived there from 1958 to 1985. The house was built in the 1920s by artist and architect William Penhallow Henderson for its first owner, Edwin Brooks.

545 Canyon is El Zaguan, the home of the Historic Santa Fe Foundation. The house was built in the 1850s and is open to the public.

The first of the former groceries on the walk was Percy's Market, at 621 Canyon Road. Today it is Canyon Road Fine Art, but it still looks like a grocery. It was Percy's Market from 1938 to 1972, when Percy Ortiz died. In addition to groceries, Percy's had gasoline pumps, so you could fill up your tank right on Canyon Road.

630 Canyon is the Olive Rush studio. Artist Olive Rush was a Quaker who moved to Santa Fe in 1920 and died in 1966. She bequeathed her home to the Religious Society of Friends to serve as a Friends meetinghouse.

653 Canyon has been The Compound Restaurant since opened it opened in 1971. It was Santa Fe's first, and for many years, only elegant restaurant. In the 1970s it was the place to go in Santa Fe for fine food and white glove service. It was tightly associated with Victor Sagheer, its perfectly mannered manager, who purchased it from the original owners in the late 1970s. After owning and managing it for 33 years, Sagheer sold The Compound in 2000 to new owners who modernized it and maintained its reputation for distinctive fine dining. The history is described on www.compoundrestaurant.com.

Before its incarnation as a restaurant, the Compound was the centerpiece of a group of houses on Canyon Road known as the McComb Compound. In the earlier part of the 20th century, when

Santa Fe was a long way from the rest of the world, movie stars, industrialists, and socialites visited, where they could rent a house in relative seclusion. Eventually, Will and Barbara Houghton acquired the main house and converted it into a restaurant. It was their decision to bring in designer Alexander Girard, who gave The Compound Restaurant its distinctive look.

Prior to 1971, it was a private residence belonging to the McComb family. David McComb arrived in Santa Fe in 1921 with his wife, Sara Meade Woolfolk. David died in 1934, and Sara remained at the house until her death in 1963. Both are buried at Fairview Cemetary.

Claude's Bar was a raucous bar at 656 Canyon Road. Today the address belongs to Tresa Vorenberg Goldsmiths. Claude James opened the bar and restaurant in the late 1950s and closed it in 1973. Claude was a hard-drinking lesbian who attracted a rough crowd. A blogger named Johnny Mango wrote this about the bar: "Back in 1970 Claude's Bar was probably the wildest place in New Mexico... it attracted such a mix of cowboys, Indians, Chicanos, artists and writers, freaks, politicians, and full-time road warriors that every night was a total eruption of fists." Claude's closed after neighbors complained of building code violations.

The former Gormley's Market, at 670 Canyon Road, was the last of the three groceries to close, in 1987. The building is now an art gallery, but in homage to its history, the name Gormley's is still painted on the building in two-foot-high letters. In 1988 the Historic Design Review Board ruled that a then 80-year-old barn behind Gormley's cannot be razed, despite owner's claims that the building is hazardous.

Until the mid-1970s there were only a handful of serious galleries on Canyon Road. One of those was Jean Seth's gallery, which opened in June 1967 at 710 Canyon Road. Jean Seth's gallery showed work by American Indians, the Taos School, Spanish colonial work, and so on. Seth closed her gallery and retired in 1988.

Geronimo Restaurant at 724 Canyon opened in 1990 in the historic Borrego house. The building was built in 1753, then remodeled in 1846 to become one of the first territorial style buildings in Santa Fe. In 1961 the house became a coffeehouse called Three Cities of Spain, which remained popular for 15 years until it closed in 1976, hosting folk singers, movies on Friday nights, and the occasional evening of live theater. Since then it's always been a restaurant. From 1977 to 1979 it was Ernie's, from 1980 to 1985 it was Alfonso's, and from 1986 to 1990 it was The Carriage Trade.

The house at 729 Canyon Road, now Chalk Farm Gallery, was the home of a prominent local preservationist, Irene von Horvath, from 1954 to 1984. Von Horvath was the last living member of the committee that authored the 1957 Historic Zoning Ordinance when she died in 2007.

At this point, Camino del Monte Sol branches off to the right. The astonishing Rio Wood Yard, on Camino del Monte Sol, was started in the 1940s by Jesus and Teresa Rios, and is still run today by their grandson, Rudy Rios. They bought the lot when they purchased the house at 324 Camino del Monte Sol from the widow of artist Frank Applegate.

In 1921, five artists who lived on Camino del Monte Sol started a collective called Los Cinco Pintores (The Five Painters) and sometimes exhibited as a group. Their principal painting style was impressionist. They were Willard Nash, Walter Mruk, Will Shuster, Josef Bakos, and Fremont Ellis. Today their homes, with addresses from 538 to 586, express authentic Spanish-Pueblo Revival. Shuster lived at 550. Mruk lived at 555. Bakos built the house at 576 Camino del Monte Sol in 1923 and lived there many years. Ellis lived at 586 ½ (until 1958).

At the top of Monte Sol (but too far to walk), is The Immaculate Heart of Mary Seminary. This was the location of Sunmount Sanitorium, a group of cottages, founded in 1903 and closed in 1970. It was a place for people with respiratory diseases such as tuberculois to recuperate. It was named for nearby Sun Mountain. When its owner died the land was sold to the Archdiocese of Santa Fe, which established the seminary. The architect John Gaw Meem and several of the artists now credited with making Santa Fe an artists' town originally came to Santa Fe specifically because of Sunmount. Those artists include poet Alice Corbin, writer Mary Austin, writer Witter Bynner, photographer Carlos Vierra, and the painters Gerald Cassidy, Sheldon Parsons, and William Penhallow Henderson.

Back on Canyon Road, pause at the corner of Canyon Road and Monte Sol and notice the corner building, which today is occupied by an art gallery. From the 1940s to 1963, this was the location of the legendary Canyon Road Bar, owned by Frank Serna. In 1963, Canyon Road Bar closed and replaced by El Farol, whose original owners were Vint Blackburn and Bob Young. In the early 1970s, El Farol moved next door to the location where it stands today. After El Farol left the corner location, a long succession of failed restaurants occupied the space until it became an art gallery in 2010.

Friendly's Market was at 830 Canyon Road, a location that today is the art studio of Eli Levin. Levin has been in Santa Fe since 1964 and in 2008, he published his memories of the artist scene in a book called *Santa Fe Bohemia: The Art Colony 1964 - 1980*. In 1981 Levin founded an artist group called the Santa Fe Etching Club, which is still going strong today.

One of the first artists to move to Santa Fe was Gerald Cassidy, who bought the house at 922 Canyon Road in 1915 and lived there until his death in 1934. The house was renovated in 2011 and was the subject of a front-page news article in *The New Mexican* in that year.

Christo Rey Church, one of the great buildings designed by John Gaw Meem, opened in 1940. It has a steel frame, so it's not a true adobe, though it has approximately 180,000 adobe bricks in its walls.

Across from Christo Rey Church there is the newly built Power Plant Park, which opened in 2010. The park contains a small museum, a 100-kilowatt hydroelectric turbine, and a five-million gallon water tank.

About 5,000 acre-feet of Santa Fe River water per year are treated at the Canyon Road Water Treatment Plant, located 1.5 miles north of the park. The water flows downhill, spins the turbine, and then either goes into the storage tank or flows down river, depending on whether the tank is full. The original hydroelectric plant on this location was in operation from 1890 to 1930.

Next door to Christo Rey Church is the old Manderfield Elementary School, which opened in the late 1920s and closed in 1972 when Atalaya Elementary opened. It was designed by John Gaw Meem and was used as a Head Start preschool from the mid-1990s to 2010.

You can skip the upper half of Canyon Road, though it is a magnificent, winding old residential road that has hardly changed in the last 100 years. In 1847, at the top of Canyon Road, three miles from the Plaza, the U.S. Army built a stone sawmill to provide lumber for the construction of Fort Marcy. In 1920 the sawmill was purchased by artist Randall Davey. He renovated and expanded the sawmill to convert it into his home. Davey was known for his lavish dinner parties and love for horse racing. He lived there until he died in 1964 at age 77. His family remained there until 1983, when they donated it to the Audubon Society. It now serves as Audubon's state headquarters.

From Christo Rey Church, walk back down Canyon Road 0.25 mile, veer left on Acequia Madre and walk 0.5 mile on Acequia Madre

Winding Acequia Madre Street follows the path of the 18th century water ditch called the Acequia Madre, meaning mother ditch. Its purpose was to irrigate gardens and orchards and to water farm animals.

After 0.4 mile, you will come to 512 Acequia Madre, a small house with wrought iron over the windows. This was the original location of Tito's Market, a tienda or neighborhood grocery, and a popular gathering place on the east-side until the 1970s. In its later years, it moved into a new building across the street, which is now the location of Downtown Subscription and Garcia Street Books. Tito's was a family business with Tito Griego usually running the cash register. His son Phil Griego, who bagged groceries and stocked shelves, is a state senator today. In 1981, after Tito's closed (at what is now Downtown Subscription), the site became the home La Tienda, a women's clothing store that had previously been on West San Francisco Street. In 1990, La Tienda closed and Downtown Subscription moved in.

At the end of Acequia Madre Street, there is a small compound of about 10 houses called Plaza Chamisal. It was built in the 1920s and '30s by Judge Miguel Otero and his wife, Katherine Stinson Otero (1893 - 1977), one of the first female aviators.

When Acequia Madre intersects Paseo de Peralta, walk along Paseo de Peralta

When you reach Paseo de Peralta, you'll turn left and walk along Paseo de Peralta. However, first look left at Gerald Peters Gallery, which is Santa Fe's largest gallery at 32,000 square feet. This Pueblo-style building was built in 1997-98. The gallery first opened in 1971 in a former residence at 439 Camino del Monte Sol.

The huge, territorial-style PERA Building (Public Employees Retirement Assocation) was constructed from 1964 to 1967. Previous to its contruction, the site and its surrounding parking lot was a Spanish and Indian graveyard, and athletic fields and tennis courts for St. Michael's High School. The graveyard operated from the 1700s to 1914, according to an article in the June 26, 1966 *New Mexican*. Note the few remaining old houses on the south side of Paseo de Peralta. These are a glimpse of the old barrio that was leveled in the early 1960s to allow for construction of the Roundhouse and the PERA Building.

Pause when you reach the corner of Paseo de Peralta and Old Santa Fe Trail. At the southeast corner is a small strip of shops built in 1955, officially known as Dos Caminos. The anchor store is Kaune's Neighborhood Market. Until 2009, the store was named Kaune Foodtown, and stated on its exterior signage "Since 1896," the date Harry S. Kaune first opened the store on the Plaza. Harry S. Kaune's granddaughter, Julie Kaune, owned and managed the store from 1971 to 1983. In 1983 she sold it to a new owner not related to the family. Today it is owned by Cheryl Pick Sommer.

The vacant lot across from Kaune's (the southwest corner of the intersection) has been vacant since 1995. Prior to that it was Capitol Chevron, a full-service gas station built in 1960 and closed in 1994.

THE SOUTH CAPITOL NEIGHBORHOOD

To the south (left on Old Santa Fe Trail) lies the South Capitol neighborhood. It's off our path quite a bit, so no walking tour is given. However, it's worth mentioning a few historical items.

The streets and homes of the South Capitol neighborhood were built in the 1920s and '30s. In this period, Pueblo-revival was not yet fully in vogue for private homes, and many of the area's houses exhibit the Arts and Crafts Bungalow style of architecture, with setbacks and small front yards. One of the city's five official historic districts, called the Don Gaspar Area Historic District, lies within the South Capitol neighborhood.

Santa Fe had a junior high school called Harrington Junior High that closed in 1978 when Capshaw Middle School opened. It was located in the South Capitol district, on the site presently occupied by the playground for Wood Gormley Elementary School. Wood Gormley opened in 1927 and is the oldest school building still in use in Santa Fe School District.

The Witter Bynner House, on E. Buena Vista Street at the corner of Old Santa Fe Trail, is one of the city's history-rich treasures.[5] The house was originally built in the 1830s. For more than 40 years it was the home of poet and bon vivant Witter Bynner. Bynner purchased the house in the 1920s and made several additions. He was famous for many things, including the wild parties he threw there. Since 1997 the house has served as an 11-room bed and breakfast called The Turquoise Bear.

OLD SANTA FE TRAIL

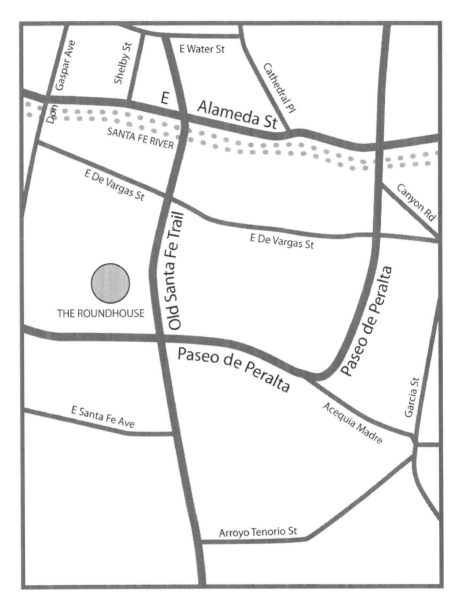

👣 *Turn right on Old Santa Fe Trail, walk to Alameda*

The state capitol, known as the Roundhouse, was completed in 1966. This area previously was a residential, working-class neighborhood. You can catch glimpses of what the neighborhood looked like on East DeVargas Street, on the block where the Playhouse Theater is located, and by the few remaining old houses that you passed on Paseo de Peralta.

Construction of the Roundhouse eliminated a residential street called Paloma Street that ran north from what was then Manhattan St. (now Paseo de Peralta). It began roughly at the location of the ramp to the Roundhouse underground garage.

Prior to 1966, the state capitol was the building on Galisteo now called the Bataan Building. The building was constructed in 1900 and served as the capitol from 1900 to 1966. In the mid 1950's the building underwent a major renovation, which totally changed the appearance of the building, to its current Territorial style. In the 1970's the building underwent another major renovation, which modified the interior of the building.

Across from the Roundhouse is the Lamy Building, the home of St. Michael's High School from 1859 to 1967. In 1859, the Christian Brothers, a Lasallian teacher order, came to Santa Fe at the request of Bishop Lamy to open St. Michael's College, a grade school. Although called a "college," St. Michael's always served elementary and high school boys. In the early decades there as also a college program, which was dropped after World War I. In 1947 the school changed its name to St. Michael's High School. In 1967 the school moved to a new home on Siringo Road, which was then a remote location on the southern edge of town. In the 1968-69 school year, following the closure of Loretto Academy, St. Michael's became co-ed, accepting girls for the first time. Old Santa Fe Trail was named College Street until 1967, when St. Michael's left the Lamy Building and moved to Siringo Road.

After the Lamy Building is San Miguel Chapel, perhaps the oldest still-standing church in America, though the truth of this claim appears murky. The bones of the building date between 1610 and 1628. It was mostly destroyed in the Pueblo revolt of 1680-92. The present building was constructed in 1710 with two major restorations since the original construction, in 1887 and in 1955-57. The altar screen dates to 1798. The church still offers mass on Sunday mornings.

Next is the The Pink Adobe, opened in 1944 by Rosalea Murphy, a legend in Santa Fe in those days. Later in her life, she described Santa Fe in the 1940s and '50s as a "lazy, sleepy town."[6]

Behind the Lamy Building is the Lew Wallace Building, built in 1887 as a dormitory for St. Michael's College. Lew Wallace was governor of the Territory of New Mexico from 1878 to 1881. Today the building serves as offices for the State Engineer and the Office of Tourism.

Garrett's Desert Inn was built in 1956 on the site of Orchard Camp, a group of cabins set among cottonwood trees, and the Orchard Camp Restaurant, a hamburger joint. The cabins were rented to tourists but had become dilapidated. Tragically, a small forest of cottonwoods was felled to built the motel.

Old Santa Fe Trail was a section of the famed Route 66 from 1926, when Route 66 was first established, until 1937. In late 1937, a new, straight section of Route 66 was laid from Santa Rosa to Albuquerque, thus bypassing Santa Fe. There are several signs along Old Santa Fe Trail and Galisteo Street that proclaim "Pre-1937 Route 66."

THE SANTA FE RIVER

Prior to the 1940s, the Santa Fe River was a healthy, flowing river. After that, dams and acequias drained it dry most of the year. In 2007 it was named America's most endangered river by American Rivers, a conservation group.

The headwaters are at Santa Fe Lake, by Lake Peak in the Sangre de Christos, at 12,408 feet. It flows into the Rio Grande River at Cochiti Lake. From headwaters to Cochiti it flows 246 miles, but the river proper is only 46 miles long. Today the river supplies about 40% of the city's water supply.

Watershed experts are unsure if the river was, prior to dams and acequias, perennial. The Santa Fe River was first dammed in 1881. That dam, called the Old Stone Dam, filled with silt during a flash flood in 1904. It is now within the 188-acre Santa Fe Canyon Preserve, managed by the Nature Conservancy. The entrance to the Preserve, which has a hiking trail and parking lot, is located at the top of Canyon Road.

Today there are two dams on the river. Nichols Dam was built in 1926 - 28 and McClure Dam was built in 1941 - 42.

In 2009 the city's Public Utilities Committee, which is a committee of the city council, passed a nonbinding resolution that the reservoirs should release a small volume of water, sufficient to maintain a steady flow, from April 1 to September 30.

Turn left on Alameda Street, walk ¼ mile along the river to Sandoval Street

Walk along the Santa Fe River. At Shelby Street, on the corner, there is a restaurant called Amavi, which opened in 2007 and replaced a restaurant called Julian's. Before Julian's took the space, it was a private home. In the 1950s and '60s, it was the home of the stately and well-known gentlemen named Gregorio Real. Mr. Real walked everywhere with a cane, wore spats, a hat, and was described as "Lincoln-like" by one resident.

Turn left on Sandoval Street. In 2008, the 40-year-old Sandoval Street bridge at West Alameda Street was torn down and replaced with a new bridge, which is identical to the old bridge. The old bridge was structurally unsound.

The pitched-roof building at 312 Sandoval Street, built in 1886, was originally a two-room schoolhouse called the Second Ward School.[7] In 1900 its exterior brick was covered with plaster, which remains today. The building served as a school until 1932, when it was replaced by the newly built Alvord School on Hickox Street. In 1936 the building was sold to Union Protectiva, a private club, which has owned the building ever since. From 1974 to 1984 it was leased to a gun shop called The Buffalo Hunter, which is now located on Airport Road and called Tina's Range Gear. After the Buffalo Hunter moved, the building became Anahita Gallery, an importer of Asian furnishings. In 2007 Anahita moved to Canyon Road and the old Second Ward School was left vacant. In 2008 the building was renovated to serve as the new home for Union Protectiva.

The building at 328 Sandoval, now Primo Cigar, looks modern but is an adobe dating to the 18th century. It housed a dry cleaner called Master Cleaners for 45 years, from 1960 to 2005, and had been owned and operated for the entire 45 years by James Salazar. In 2007 the building was gutted and renovated. A bed and bath shop called Casa Natura occupied the building for two years, from 2007 to 2009.

The construction site at the corner of Sandoval and Montezuma is the former site of The Paramount, a popular nightclub from 1998 to 2005. A smaller attached building contained a swank lounge called Bar B. It was a big loss for Santa Fe nightlife when the two spots closed in 2005. The owner sold the building to Santa Fe County, which is building a courthouse. The building was vacant for three years until it was razed in 2008. That building was originally built in 1988 as architectural offices, then in 1995 was renovated and transformed into a high-end restaurant called the Double-A, which closed in 1997 after less than two years in business. Groundbreaking for the new courthouse occurred in November 2008. Originally, construction was scheduled for completion in 2010, but after underground gasoline contamination was discovered, completion was delayed to 2013.

The building at 418 Sandoval, now called The Design Center, was built in 1932 to serve as Santa Fe's Chevrolet dealership. The dealership remained there until the 1980s when the Auto Park opened at the lower end of Cerrillos Road. The building across the street at 428 Sandoval that looks like a garage and currently is home to Copy Shack was the dealership's repair garage.

515 Cerrillos Road, now dilapidated, was constructed in 1943 as Hancock Oldsmobile, an auto dealership. Hancock Olds lasted for 28 years before closing in 1971. The next year the building was converted into a stationary store called Healy-Matthews Stationers. That business remained open until 1989, and today the building is known as the Healy-Matthews Building. From 2000 to 2002 the building was rented by Open Hands, a thrift store. Since Open Hands moved out, the building has been vacant except for occasional use as a theater for plays.

519 Cerrillos Road was constructed in 1948 as a movie theater called the Santa Fe Theatre. In those days this was an unusual location for movies since the town's three established theaters -- the Lensic, the El Paseo, and the Alley -- were all on East San Francisco Street. Santa Fe Theatre lasted only nine years before closing in 1957. The building was absorbed into Hancock Oldsmobile. A disco called Club Cargo occupied the building from 1989 to 1992, which was then replaced by popular nightclub, Club Luna, which lasted only two years before closing in 1994. In 2011-12 the building was renovated as a live/work building with retail shops.

Hotel Santa Fe opened in 1991 on a seven-acre site at the corner of Cerrillos and Paseo de Peralta. This site was previously a mobile home park called Covered Wagon Trailer Court, and a series of stores, some of which were around for decades. Frank's Lounge was there at 530 Cerrillos from 1961 until it closed in 1979. David's Portrait Studio at 544 Cerrillos was a photography studio that still operates on Airport Road under a new name, Images by David. Mountain Bell, the phone company, was there. The largest building on the site had originally (in the late 19th century) been the Frances Willard School for Girls, which was the only school west of the Mississippi River operated by the Women's Christian Temperance Union. Around 1918 the property was acquired by the Bonal family, which owned it until about 1989. For 70 years the Bonals owned and operated most of the businesses on the site.

When you reach Paseo de Peralta, turn right and walk toward Community Bank

This section of Paseo de Peralta was a two-lane section of Hickox Street until about 1972. When you reach Community Bank, cut through the parking lot. Walk to the railroad tracks on the side of the building. Then look down into the crevice below. You will see a massive block of carved stone. This is a section of the old railroad turntable used by two railroads, the Chili Line and New Mexico Central. It was uncovered when Community Bank was built. The turntable was used to turn locomotives around when they reached the end of the line. Oddly, no plaque marks this remarkable site.

GUADALUPE

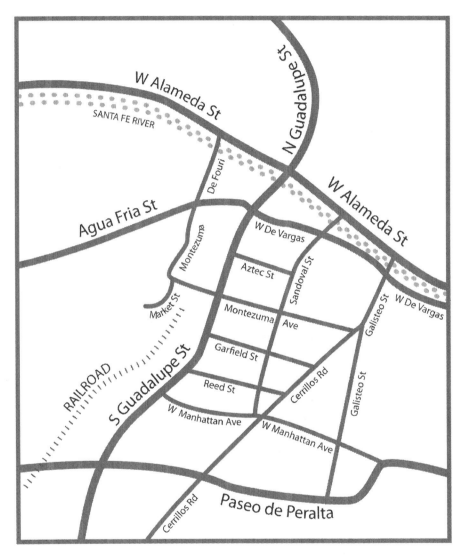

👣 *Turn right on Guadalupe Street*

Guadalupe Street will take us into Santa Fe's Guadalupe district and the railyard. But first, look left (but don't walk left) along Guadalupe St. Today Guadalupe Street intersects Cerrillos Road at the Allsup's/Shell. But until the mid-1970s, Guadalupe Street did not extend south of Hickox Street. Old railroad tracks in that area were torn out to permit the extension of Guadalupe Street from Hickox to Cerrillos.

Now turn right (north) on Guadalupe Street, which lines the 47-acre railyard. The Gross Kelly Warehouse in the railyard was built in 1913, the first commercial building in Santa Fe designed in Spanish-Pueblo Revival style. It was a warehouse for goods transported into town on the railroad. The building was constructed parallel to the railroad tracks for easy loading and unloading. In the 1990s the building was dilapidated and marred by additions and modifications. It was purchased and renovated in 2000 - 01 by David Barker to serve as offices for Barker Realty. The renovation included restoration and preservation of the building's original components and design.

Tomasita's Restaurant, a red-brick building, was built in 1903 as the depot for two railroads, the Chili Line and New Mexico Central. It has been home to Tomasita's Restaurant since 1981.

Across from Tomasita's at 435 Guadalupe is a 1920s building at 435 S. Guadalupe that is home to several art galleries. In 2007 the building's interior was demolished and rebuilt, while the exterior front was preserved and restored to its original appearance.

After Tomasita's, you'll see the city's first train depot, built in 1880 and constructed in Mission Revival style with a red-tile roof. It was built for the Atchison, Topeka & Santa Fe (AT&SF) Railway. It stands today, almost exactly as it was built, and still serves as a passenger depot. Today the city owns the building and leases it to Santa Fe Southern Railway, which took over freight service in 1993 and reintroduced passenger service.

The five-story Italianate building with the mansard roof at 330 Garfield Street was built in 1882 by a Congregationalist Christian school called the University of New Mexico (no relation to today's University of New Mexico in Albuquerque). In the early 20th Century it became a hotel called The Franciscan Hotel, which occupied the building for decades. Today the building is known as University Plaza and serves as offices for BGK Properties Inc., a real estate investment firm.

Keep walking until you reach Montezuma Street, then look to the left, toward Sanbusco Center. The building on the corner with address 328 S. Guadalupe contains about five retail shops, one of which was Sangre de Cristo Mountain Works, facing Montezuma Street, which sold camping and hiking gear from 1994 to 2011.

Keep walking until you reach Aztec Street, then pause. At the corner of Aztec and Guadalupe, we're standing on the 300 block of Guadalupe Street. This block is remarkable for its intact railroad-era buildings. Most were built as warehouses, except Cowgirl, which was a flophouse for people who just arrived off the train. Today those warehouses are used by Zia Diner, Cielo, Café Dominic, DoubleTake, and Gypsy Baby. In the mid-20th century, these buildings were in poor condition and mostly used by auto repair shops. Retail stores did not arrive on Guadalupe Street until the 1970s. Cowgirl restaurant opened on June 1, 1993; the site had previously served as several other restaurants.

The brick-fronted building at 316 Guadalupe Street, now occupied by Cielo Bed and Bath, is officially known as the Stone Warehouse. It was built in 1885, shortly after the railroad arrived.

320 Guadalupe, which has been Café Dominic since 2000, was the Swiss Bakery from 1976 to 1995, which baked wonderful French pastry

and served espresso. Then it became Atalaya Restaurant, which closed in 1999.

326 Guadalupe has been Zia Diner since 1986, when it was opened by Beth and Bernhard Draiscol, who still own it today. Before Zia Diner opened, it was an auto body repair shop called (starting in 1973) Supreme Body Shop and (prior to 1973) Max and Richard's Body Shop. Originally the building was a coal warehouse built in the late 1800s.

Walk down Aztec Street to Aztec Street Café, which opened in March 1990. The building was originally constructed as a bunkhouse for railroad workers, probably around 1885 to 1900.

At the corner of Guadalupe Street and Agua Fria, we see El Santuario de Guadalupe. The church was built in 1960. It replaced a smaller church on the same site. From 1609 until Gen. Stephen Kearny arrived in 1846, this church marked the northern tip of the Camino Real, which was the Santa Fe's connection to the outside world all those years.

Next to the church is Keller Williams Realty. Prior to 2009, the building was occupied by two businesses, Southwest Spanish Craftsmen and Nussbaumer Fine Art. The building was built in the early 1920s as the parochial elementary school attached to the Santuario de Guadalupe.

Reverse one block on Guadalupe, turn right on Montezuma, walk to Sanbusco

For 95 years, from 1881 to 1976, the site of Sanbusco Center it was a lumber yard and building materials company. It sold lumber, doors and windows, and roofing. The original business was constructed by Charles Dudrow in 1881, who selected the location because it was the terminus of the railroad, which transported building supplies. Following his death in 1910 and transfer to new ownership, the business was named Santa Fe Builders Supply Co., known popularly as Sanbusco. It expanded during the 1920s, '30s, and '40s, then went into a slow decline. By the 1970s it had become dilapidated, with boarded windows and peeling paint. It was acquired and renovated by Joe Schepps in 1984 to become a shopping center. Inside by the restrooms are wonderful photographs of the old Sanbusco lumber yard.

For 13 years, from 1997 to 2011, the anchor tenant at Sanbusco was a Borders Bookstore. The store closed in March 2011 when the company declared bankruptcy.

One of the owners of the post-1910 Sanbusco was Charles Proebstel. Proebstel built his home in 1928 at 540 East Alameda, today a splendid and unique property known as the Delgado-Spiegel property. The exterior has a California Mission motif, which is similar to Spanish-Pueblo Revival, but with a peaked roof of red tile and doorframes and doors with rounded arches.

Next door to Sanbusco is a 1930s territorial style building, the Butler & Foley Building. It is home to Cost Plus and several smaller businesses. Originally it was Eubank Lumber and Supply Co. Then it served as the Butler & Foley Plumbing Company from 1944 to 1984, when Joe Schepps purchased and renovated the building to restore its 1930s appearance.

Walk through the Borders parking lot to enter the railyard. The building facing the parking lot labeled Block Mercantile was originally the railroad's meat locker. Meat delivered by train was stored in the building prior to its distribution to grocers.

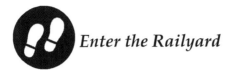 *Enter the Railyard*

The railyard had been mostly a huge vacant lot ever since the Chili Line stopped running in 1941. It was a desolate, rutted dirt lot, a no-man's land bisected by railroad tracks. In 1995 the City of Santa Fe purchased the 47-acre railyard through a voter-approved bond. There were 10 drawn-out years before groundbreaking on the redevelopment in 2005.

Prior to redevelopment of the railyard, there were a handful of ramshackle warehouses. There was the Gross Kelly warehouse, Site Santa Fe, El Museo, Warehouse 21 (which was razed and replaced by the new Warehouse 21), the Performance Center, the Sears warehouse and a neighboring warehouse that was razed in 2007. At that time, the only new building in the railyard was the office building of *Outside* magazine, built in the early 1990s. The railyard's grand opening occurred in September 2008. The new buildings follow a master plan dictate that they be designed to reflect "the warehouse, industrial and commercial history of the site and the concept of an arts and cultural district."

It was a coincidence that redevelopment of the railyard (2005 - 2008) occurred simultaneously with extension of the Road Runner commuter train from Bernalillo to Santa Fe (2006 - 2008). The railyard is one of four train stations constructed in Santa Fe for the Road Runner. Service began in December 2008 but the Rail Runner made a symbolic run to the railyard at its grand opening on September 13, 2008.

The building now occupied by Site Santa Fe was the warehouse for Maloof Distributing, a Coors beer distributor. The warehouse closed in the late 1970s. Site Santa Fe, an exhibition space for contemporary art, moved into the building in 1995.

The railyard building directly across from Site Santa Fe was originally built as a warehouse for Sears Roebuck. In the 1990s it was a ramshackle building used by a packing and shipping business called Boxes, Bubbles, and Beans. In 2006 it was gutted and renovated to serve as one of three art galleries now known as the Railyard Galleries complex. The other two art galleries were entirely new construction, and replaced an existing warehouse.

The Farmers' Market building (olive green color) and Market Station (home of REI and other retail stores) were constructed in 2007 - 08. The Truro Building (facing Warehouse 21) was constructed in 2009.

The railyard is the last easily walkable area of Santa Fe. From here you can continue walking, though many will prefer to drive.

THE AUTOMOBILE ARRIVES VIA CERRILLOS ROAD IN THE 1930S

It was not until the 1930s that the automobile became the predominant way for people to reach Santa Fe.

Cars entered Santa Fe on Cerrillos Road. The lower half of Cerrillos Road was called the Albuquerque Highway until the 1970s when it was renamed Cerrillos Road. Cerrillos Road was a two-lane road until the 1960s, when it was widened to four lanes. In 1932, the last address on Cerrillos Road was the U.S. Indian School. Beyond that was nothing but an empty road.

In the 1930s the automobile was quickly becoming popular, replacing the railroad as the principal way for people to reach Santa Fe. Service stations and motels known as "auto courts" sprang up along Cerrillos Road in the later 1930s, establishing it as the ugly commercial strip that it remains today. Some of the motels remain in operation today. As of 2007 many of the older motels are still operating in run-down condition: Desert Chateau Motel, Western Scene Motel, Cottonwood Court, Silver Saddle Motel, Stage Coach Motor Inn, Kings Rest Court Inn, Thunderbird Inn. Just one of the old motor courts has been well-maintained and remains a good place to stay: The El Rey Inn, which opened in 1936 as a 12-room motor court. It now has 86 rooms.

Driving Down Cerrillos Road

The drive down Cerrillos Road begins at the corner of Cerrillos and Paseo de Peralta. The retail building at 607 Cerrillos Road that houses a pet store was constructed in the 1980s. Previously the site was home to Cherry Motor Co., a Cadillac dealership, which closed in the 1970s.

The vacant lot at 631 Cerrillos, between Don Diego and Paseo de Peralta, was for 50 years a gas station called Jimmie's Quick Stop. It closed in 1998. In 2000 a developer proposed a retail/office building for the site, but neighbors objected to the three-story height and the developer abandoned the project.

Whole Foods opened on a five-acre site on Cerrillos Road in 2000. Previously the site was a lumber yard called Houston Lumber. When it first opened it had insufficient space for parking. Next door was an aging McDonald's. In 2006 that McDonald's was razed to create an overflow parking lot for Whole Foods. The McDonald's franchisee built a new restaurant a few hundred yards south on St. Francis, on the site of a former JB's Restaurant.

The mini-strip mall at the corner of St. Francis and Cerrillos was called Pen Road Shopping Center until 2008, when the owner changed its name to Crossroads Center "because no one know where Pen Road was." Pen Road used to run on both sides of what became St. Francis Drive, but now ends on the southwest side of St. Francis. The strip mall was built in the late 1950s. Tiny's Lounge has been located in the strip mall since 1971.

Tin Nee Ann, a tourist shop for Indian crafts, opened in 1973. That structure was a private home until 1968. At that time the house was acquired by a couple who, previous to that date, had owned a

Kirby vacuum cleaner business on the Five Points location, which was destroyed by the 1968 flood. They purchased the house, divided it in two, and transformed it into a vacuum repair shop and an H&R Block. In 1973, with tourists eager for Indian crafts, they changed it into Tin Nee Ann.

New Mexico School for the Deaf was founded privately in 1885, and then became a state-owned school through an act of the state legislature in 1887. It sits on a 30-acre campus at the corner of Cerrillos and St. Francis Drive. It has 150 students in grades kindergarten through 12. The campus was designed by the firm of Rapp & Rapp in approximately 1917. The three-story Connor Hall, built in 1928 as a boys' dormitory, was gutted and reopened in 2010 as a career and technical education center.

Fairview Cemetery on Cerrillos Road is the burial place containing more than 3,700 graves, including those of many prominent Santa Feans. Ralph Emerson Twitchell, artists Gerald Cassidy and Frank Applegate, six members of the Catron family, and 11 members of the Seligman family are buried there. The cemetery was founded on May 7, 1884 but its earliest gravestones date from 1862 because some graves were moved from a Masonic graveyard on the north side of downtown in 1883-84. Today it is owned by the Fairview Cemetery Preservation Association. It is the city's oldest non-Catholic cemetery.

At the corner of Cerrillos and Baca Street, the site now occupied by a gas station was an iconic teenage hangout called Fred's Drive-In. In business from 1964 to 1977, Fred's Drive-In was owned by Frederick Johnson, a pioneer who was driven out of business when fast-food chains arrived in Santa Fe in the mid-1970s. "For years, it was the place to meet your friends on Friday and Saturday night to make plans and find out where that night's party was going to be," wrote *The New Mexican* in Mr. Johnson's obituary.[8]

Santa Fe Indian School was established in 1890 as an off-reservation boarding school. It occupies 115 acres along Cerrillos Road. In 1975 the Federal government passed control of the school to New Mexico's 19 pueblos, represented by the All Indian Pueblo Council, which created Santa Fe Indian School Inc. The original campus consisted of 18 brick buildings along Cerrillos Road, dated from 1890 to 1930.

In 2008, after construction of new school buildings at the rear of the property, the SFIS board of directors decided to eliminate the entire original campus. In July to September 2008, all 18 buildings were razed and hundreds of mature trees were cut down. Those buildings included classroom buildings, homes for teachers, dormitories, a gymnasium, and a bakery. They were one of the last good examples of the brick, pitched roof, Eastern-style of architecture that came west with the railroad. Santa Fe had a distinct 33-year period of architecture from 1880, when the railroad arrived, to 1913, when the Pueblo architectural revival began. Many of the SFIS buildings had been remodeled by John Gaw Meem in the 1930s to transform them into Spanish-Pueblo Revival. Interior walls of many of the buildings had New Deal-era murals.

An angry controversy arose and occupied the newspapers for more than six months. Preservationists railed against the destruction but SFIS officials maintained the school is a sovereign entity, and as such, is not subject to federal or state law.

Another significant structure on the Indian School campus was the Paolo Soleri Amphitheater, a popular outdoor event venue seating 2,700. Originally designed for Indian theater performances, it hosted countless school graduations and music performances and was considered the best venue in Santa Fe for outdoor rock concerts. It was designed in 1955 by architect Paolo Soleri but construction was not complete until 1965. In 2010 the All Indian Pueblo Council confirmed its intention to demolish the structure.

The Pantry Restaurant on Cerrillos Road opened at that same location in 1947. At that time it was on the outskirts of town. When it opened, it consisted only of the breakfast bar and front dining room; what is now the back dining room used to be the home of the family that owned it. In

2008, scenes for the movie *Crazy Heart* were filmed in The Pantry.

The first strip mall in Santa Fe was built in 1955 and called Santa Fe Shopping Center. It served the newly built Casa Alegre subdivision built across Cerrillos Road. The mall's address was 2100 Cerrillos Road, at the corner of what is now St. Michael's Drive, where Ace Hardware is located today. In the mid-70s a developer purchased 15 acres of adjacent land on Cerrillos Road from The College of Santa Fe to build a larger mall. The old mall was razed in the late 1970s and in 1980 College Plaza strip mall was built. In 1981, the developer purchased an additional 5.5 acres along Cerrillos Road from the College of Santa Fe to build a Skagg's Alpha Beta grocery store. The building occupied by Smith's supermarket has always been a supermarket but Smith's is the fifth incarnation. It started as Skagg's Alpha Beta, which closed in 1988. Then it was a Jewel-Osco, then Lucky, then Albertson's for a brief period of about two months, and then around 2000 it became Smith's, which it remains today.

In the late 1940s, a local homebuilder named Allen Stamm began building master planned subdivisions along Cerrillos Road. Stamm had started building houses in 1939 - 40 with a small number of homes in the Lovato Heights area (a block south of Cordova along Escalante and Alta Vista streets). His later projects were the first large-scale housing developments in Santa Fe. Those homes were popular and the population shifted away from the Plaza. Between 1949 and 1960 he built Casa Linda (Kaune neighborhood), Carlos Rey, Casa Alegre, Casa Solana, and Barrio La Cañada. Ultimately Stamm built about 2,800 homes in Santa Fe. The first subdivisions on the south side of town were built in the 1960s by a builder named Dale Bellamah. The Bellamah homes are primarily off Siringo Road, an arterial street that was laid out and paved in the early 1960s.

Kaune Elementary School was built in 1949 on Monterey Drive to serve the newly constructed Casa Linda neighborhood, which soon came to be known as the Kaune neighborhood. The school was closed in 2010 by the school board as a cost-cutting measure, and the building was sold for $4 million to Desert Academy, a private school.

On the exterior wall of Empire Builders at 1802 Cerrillos Road is a huge mural, completed in 1981. It is one of three murals in Santa Fe by the German expressionist painter Zara Kriegstein. Her other two murals are on the old state archives building on Guadalupe Street and inside the Municipal Court building. She lived in Santa Fe from 1973 until her death in 2009.

Silva Lanes, Santa Fe's only bowling alley, was located on Rufina Circle. It closed in December 2008 after new bowling alleys opened in Pojoaque and Espanola. The bowling alley had originally been owned by Bill Grandstaff and was known as BG's Kiva Lanes. The name was changed to Silva Lanes in 1997 when it was purchased by Art Silva. Bill Grandstaff opened Kiva Lanes after his first bowling alley, Coronado Lanes, located in the Cordova strip mall, closed in 1993 and became Leishman's Furniture. The first bowling alley in Santa Fe was Zia Lanes at 118 East Marcy Street. It had six lanes and was open from the 1930s until the early 1950s.

The Yucca Drive-In outdoor movie theater on Cerrillos Road opened in 1950 and closed in 1994. The site has become the Alameda Condos, adjacent to the Lofts. There was another drive-in movie theater called the Pueblo. In the 1950s it was located on U.S. 84/285, in the field between the mobile home court and the turnoff to the former Rancho Encantando. In the early 1960s the Pueblo moved to Cerrillos Road. It closed in the early 1980s. In 1993 - 94, Wal-Mart was constructed on the site formerly occupied by the Pueblo Drive-In. Wal-Mart's first store in Santa Fe opened in 1985 in the Cerrillos Road building now occupied by Hobby Lobby.

Villa Linda mall opened in 1985 with two anchor tenants: Mervyn's and Dillard's. The third anchor, JC Penney, waited one year until 1986 to move from its location at DeVargas Mall. The fourth anchor, Sears, moved from its downtown location in 1990. In 2006 the mall was sold to a new owner, which updated the interior and changed the name to Santa Fe Place. Mervyn's closed in 2008 when the entire national chain declared Chapter 11 bankruptcy.

Horseman's Haven Café has been located at 4354 Cerrillos Road since about 1980. Owned and operated by the Romero family, it's known for the quality and heat of its chile. The current 2,500 square foot restaurant was built in 2003 and replaced the well-worn, original 900-square foot building at the same location.

Just before Cerrillos intersects I-25, before the outlet mall at Beckner Road, there is a large development in progress. That is Los Soleras, a 545-acre mixed use project on land that was annexed by the city in 2008. The project will include homes, a school, park space, a new hospital to be built by Presbyterian Health, and a large state-owned office building.

THE RAILROAD ARRIVES IN SANTA FE IN 1880

The Atchison Topeka and Santa Fe Railroad arrived in Las Vegas, NM (then the largest city in New Mexico) in 1879. The first train into Santa Fe arrived on February 9, 1880. Previous to that, people and goods arrived by horse and carriage. The railroad to Santa Fe was a spur, not the main line. The spur came from Lamy, 18 miles to the east. Passenger service on the AT&SF was discontinued on October 1, 1926. From that date, passengers, baggage, and mail had to be transported from Lamy on buses known as Harvey cars. Freight was still carried on the AT&SF. An actual AT&SF steam locomotive manufactured in 1944 sits in Salvador Perez Park on St. Francis Drive.

In 1887, a second railroad, a narrow-gauge line, reached Santa Fe from the north. It was built by Texas, Santa Fe & Northern Railroad Co., which in 1895 sold the tracks to Denver & Rio Grande Railroad. That train, known locally as the Chili Line, ran north from the railyard, along what is now Guadalupe Street, crossing Johnson, McKenzie, Staab, and Catron Street. The Chili Line ran until 1941 when its tracks were torn out and sold to Japan (shortly before Pearl Harbor). In those decades, the Chili Line was the principal method that produce, livestock, minerals, and other products from northern New Mexico reached their markets throughout the West.

The Chili Line was a way of life for many people and old-timers remember it fondly. The tracks for the Chili Line ran 125 miles north to Colorado through cottonwood trees and cinders tossed from the locomotive. After its tracks were torn up, the track bed became Guadalupe Street. A portion of the old Denver & Rio Grande still runs today, as a tourist train called the Cumbres &

Toltec Scenic Railroad, between Chama, New Mexico and Antonito, Colorado. As with other remote locations in the west, the railroad transformed Santa Fe. It accelerated the Anglo invasion. People, language, customs, culture, architecture, business--all were changed by Santa Fe's railroads.

👣 *Driving North on Guadalupe St.*

Until 1977, Guadalupe Street's northern terminus was the "five points" intersection, one block north of Alameda Street. Today's northern section of Guadalupe St. (above Alameda St.) was Jefferson St. until 1977. Jefferson Street followed the former tracks of the Chili Line, and at McKenzie there was a Y. The left side of the Y became Rosario Street, which continued past Rosario Cemetery and merged into 84/285. The right side of the Y was East Jefferson (today simply called Jefferson). In 1977 the streets known as Jefferson and Rosario Streets were renamed Guadalupe Street, which meant that Guadalupe Street extended all the way from Cerrillos Road to 84/285.

Driving north on Guadalupe St., a man named Leonard Bertrum opened Bert's Burger Bowl at its present location in 1954, on what was then Rosario Street. Behind Bert's Burger Bowl is the UPS Store, which opened in 1991 in a building that had previously been a 7-Eleven convenience store. The gas station and retail/office building immediately to the north, currently housing the FedEx store, was the site of Capitol Motor Co., a Ford dealer, until 1980. That was the northern edge of town.

The site across the street from Bert's is Chopstix, a Chinese carry-out. Until the 1980s, that was Gene's Shamrock Service Station. Notice that the exterior still has the old shamrock colored glass and green tile.

Facing Catron Street there is a building that houses New York Deli. When it changed owners in 2010, the name changed from Bagalmania, which had opened at that location in 1991. Before Bagelmania it was a paint and body shop, and then a mechanic's garage.

Carlos Gilbert Elementary School was built in 1942 on a former railroad property where several set of railroad tracks curved and turned north. In 2009 the school underwent an $8 million remodel that added 15,000 square feet.

El Corazon, a residential condo development on Catron St., was built in 2005. Previously the site was occupied by a few dilapidated houses and the El Seville Apartments, a drab, decrepit, low-income project built in the 1950s and razed in 2003. Construction of Los Alamos National Bank at the corner of Catron and Jefferson occurred simultaneously with El Corazon. The round building on the bank's property (visible from Paseo de Peralta) was ruled to be historic and the bank restored it.

Construction on DeVargas Center, Santa Fe's first indoor mall, began in 1972. It opened in November 1973. The architect was William Lumpkins, a well-known local architect and painter. Previously the land was undeveloped and was owned by the Archdiocese of Santa Fe. The developer and original owner was Nash Hancock, a local auto dealer. He acquired the land intending to open a new auto dealership. On a trip to an auto show in Minnesota, he noticed the growing popularity of indoor shopping malls, and changed his mind. Instead of building an auto dealership, he built DeVargas Center.

The Albertson's building on the mall's north side was built in 2001. Previously the Albertson's at this mall was located in the southeast corner location facing Paseo de Peralta, next to the CVS Pharmacy. That location was vacant from 2001 through 2008. In 2009 it was gutted and reopened as Sunflower Farmers Market.

Continuing north on Guadalupe St., there are two cemeteries on the right. First is Rosario Cemetery, established in 1868 and still in use. Next is the 79-acre Santa Fe National Cemetery. According to the Veterans' Affairs website, the first burial there occurred in 1868 and the cemetery was officially established in 1875. As of 2008, more than 44,000 veterans and their spouses were buried on the cemetery.

Behind the two cemeteries you can see the tops of some abandoned buildings. That is an abandoned school that occupies 18 acres of prime real estate. It can be reached at the top of Griffin Street. St. Catherine's Indian School was founded in 1887 by Philadelphia banking heiress Katharine Drexel, a nun who earlier founded a Catholic order and named the school after a 16th century Catholic saint. It occupied an 18-acre site north of the city, next to Rosario Cemetery and Santa Fe National Cemetery. The school closed in 1998 and the site was abandoned. The city has designated eight of the 19 buildings as historic landmarks.

The following description of St. Catherine's was published on www. amandakellerkonya.com.

St. Catherine's Indian School is located in Santa Fe, New Mexico. For over one hundred years the school provided education for generations of Native American students. Katharine Drexel provided funds to build the first school building in 1887 which once housed the entire school. Throughout the school's 111-year existence enrollment increased, and the campus grew with additional buildings. Drexel continued to donate funds to the school until her death in 1995. During her lifetime Drexel also took religious vows, founded the Sisters of the Blessed Sacrament and devoted her life to educating minorities. Pope John Paul II canonized Blessed Mother Katharine in 2000.

In its later years of operation, the school continued to educate primarily Native American Indian students. In 1965 the school opened enrollment to non-Indian students. Several artists were educated at St Catherine's including painter Manuel Chavez, muralist Pablita Velarde, and potter Maria Martinez. The St. Catherine's Indian School is no stranger to closure. Prior to its most recent closure, the campus was temporarily closed from 1893 - 1894. The original closure resulted from the government's pulling the school's contract due to lack of adequate water for cultivation purposes.

After Drexel's death the Sisters of the Blessed Sacrament found it difficult to maintain appropriate religious staff and to keep up with *the school's $500,000 annual operating budget. Fundraising efforts, a lease to an independent board and a proposal for a Catholic school all failed to save St. Catherine's. In 1998 the Sisters of the Blessed Sacrament announced the school's permanent closure.*

Driving north on 84/285, in 1957 the Santa Fe Opera was built at the same location where it is today. The building was destroyed by fire in 1966. A new opera building was constructed on the same location and opened to the public in 1967. In 1998 that building was replaced by the outdoor opera that occupies the site today. John Crosby founded the Opera and served as its general director until 2000. After Crosby, the key person behind the opera was Richard Gaddes, who was with the company for 40 years, from 1968 to 2008, the last eight years as general director.

THE INTERSTATE HIGHWAY

The section of Interstate 25 between Albuquerque and Santa Fe was completed in 1973. It follows the route of the old Albuquerque Highway, a two-lane state road. When it was first built, you could not see any part of Santa Fe from the highway. By the late 1980s you could see indications of the city's southern edge from the highway. By the late 1990s building were lining the highway and had crossed to the south side of the highway.

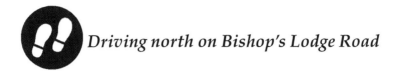 *Driving north on Bishop's Lodge Road*

Today's Fort Marcy Community Building, known as Fort Marcy gym, was constructed in 1982 on part of Magers Field (pronounced Majors). Magers Field was the football field for Santa Fe High until 1972. The baseball field on the north side of Fort Marcy park has been a baseball field since the early part of the 20th century.

Santa Fe's first condo development was built in 1971. Dubbed La Patria, it contains about 10 condos and is located at 728 Bishop's Lodge Road, across from Valley Road. These condos have no storage space because they were designed to serve as second homes. The second condo development was San Mateo of Santa Fe, which opened in 1972 at the corner of St. Francis Drive and San Mateo Road.

A high-end spa and resort in Tesuque named Encantado opened in 2008, with 65 luxury casitas, a spa, restaurant, and bar. From 1932 to 1960, the site was a dude ranch called Rancho del Monte, where horses and western life were the main attraction. The site was abandoned from 1960 to 1967. In 1968 Betty Egan, a well-known and popular local, re-opened it as a resort called Rancho Encantado. It was known for weddings, for a fun place to hang out at the bar, and for the way Betty Egan held court. She ran it until it closed in 1999. In 1999 it sold to investors who spent $40 million to built the new resort.

If you drive north on Artist Road (which changes name to Hyde Park Road), in four miles you'll arrive at Ten Thousand Waves, the Japanese-style spa, which opened in 1981. The site had been a small ranch offering horseback rides to tourists.

Driving on St. Francis Drive and the west side of town

The west side of Santa Fe, meaning to the west of Guadalupe St. and the railyard, was undeveloped until the 1920s. Alto Street and Agua Fria St. existed as dirt roads for agricultural use.

In the 1920s, a subdivision was platted to create the west side of town. Streets were established and residential construction commenced along the principal traffic corridors -- Hickox and Camino Sierra Vista. The subdivision was bordered on the north by Alto Street, on the south by Camino Sierra Vista, on the west by Camino Alire, and on the east by the railyard. These houses were designed to be inexpensive and modest in size to meet the needs of an expanding lower income population. Many of these houses are substantially unchanged, such as those on Kathryn Street and Don Juan Street.

B.F. Young Junior High School on Camino Sierra Vista was built in 1953 and operated as a junior high until 1980 when Alameda Junior High opened. Since 1980 the building has served as an administrative and training building for the school district.

The construction of a trans-city highway--the future St. Francis Drive--was first proposed in 1946. The project was controversial and delayed by disputes among property owners, developers, business owners, and other interested parties. Construction began in 1956 but was not complete until 1964. A detailed map from 1960 shows that in that year, St. Francis Drive was a half-mile length from Cordova Road to Mercer Street. The extension of St. Francis Drive north from Mercer Street in the early 1960s bisected the west side of town and absorbed several smaller streets including Doroteo, Marquita, and Gilberton. It largely destroyed the unified character of the west side and today, many west side streets remain dilapidated.

In 2009, a 104-unit public housing complex on West Alameda Street called Villa Alegre was razed. It was located on two non-continguous lots, a total of 10 acres separated by the Salvation Army building, just off St. Francis Drive. Villa Alegre had been built in 1964 and become dilapidated and overgrown with weeds. Construction for a new low-income housing complex was completed in 2011, creating 139 mixed-income units managed by Santa Fe Civic Housing Authority.

The small building on Hickox St. that houses Tune-Up Café was a burger joint called Dave's Not Here from 1981 to 2007. Tune-Up Café renovated the interior and opened for business in 2008. From 1973 to 1981, the building served as the original location of Tomasita's Restaurant.

One of Santa Fe's early movie theaters, the Arco Theater, opened in 1948 on Hickox Street across from St. Anne Catholic Church.

In an ugly episode in Santa Fe's history, during World War II there was a Japanese internment camp off West Alameda. Shortly after Pearl Harbor, the U.S. Justice Department (not the War Department) purchased the 80-acre site, which had been a CCC camp originally built in 1933. The War Relocation Authority opened the camp on March 14, 1942. It was known as the "Jap Camp." The internees were mostly first generation Japanese Americans. The maximum number of internees at any one time was 2,100 and the total number of people incarcerated there was 4,555. There were 15 barracks buildings in the camp, basically wood and tar paper shacks, surrounded by a sturdy fence. The camp closed in April 1946. Camp Santa Fe was one of 10 Japanese internment camps in the U.S. during that period that held a total of 110,000 people. After the war, a residential subdivision, Casa Solana, was constructed on the site, which erased all trace of the internment camp. In 2002, a plaque was installed on a boulder in Frank Ortiz Park, overlooking Casa Solana, to commemorate the wartime experiences of the internees.

SPECIAL EVENTS: LAS FIESTAS & INDIAN MARKET

Zozobra celebrations--the annual burning of an effigy of gloom--started in Santa Fe in 1924. Back then it was three feet tall and only people in the neighborhood knew about it. It was burned in an open field located between what is now the Main Library and the building that houses The Santa Fe Reporter. In 1939 or 1940 Zozobra moved to Fort Marcy, and it has burned there every September since that time. Now it is 49 feet tall and about 20,000 people attend. Will Schuster (1893-1969), a local artist, created Zozobra for the annual Fiesta. Schuster signed over the copyright and trademark to the Kiwanis Club in 1964.

Indian Market, a two-day annual event held in September, began in 1921 as a part of tourism and to help Natives assimilate. It remained a minor event until the late 1960s, when art collectors focused on Indian pottery, jewelry, baskets, beadwork, painting, and sculpture. Indian Market grew rapidly, prices of the art skyrocketed, prize money increased substantially, and Indian artists from all over the U.S. began to participate. It is sponsored by Southwest Association for Indian Arts.

St. Michael's Drive

St. Michael's Drive was paved and developed in the 1960s. It existed prior to that time as a dirt road. On a 1955 map of Santa Fe, it was labeled "truck bypass" but by the time a 1959 map was published, it was referred to as St. Michael's Drive. Once it was paved it immediately it became a two-mile length of strip malls and car dealerships. The strip mall called St. Michael's Village West was built in the late 1960s. The Green Onion Tavern, a blue-collar bar, opened in 1973 and closed in 2008 after 35 years in business. Before 1973 the building was a bar called the Bottle and Glass.

The first car dealership to open on St. Michael's Drive was Sauter Lincoln-Mercury, opened by Henry Sauter in 1965. It was just off Cerrillos Road at 1500 St. Michael's Drive. Henry Sauter's roots in the car business in Santa Fe reached back to the 1920s. Sauter added Toyota to his line of autos in 1966, and eventually the dealership was renamed Sauter Toyota.

Michael Beaver purchased the dealership from the Sauter family in 2002 and renamed the business Beaver Toyota.

After World War II, the Christian Brothers wanted to expand into higher education, believing Santa Fe needed a four-year college. In 1947 they purchased the majority of the site of the former Bruns Army Hospital, a World War II veterans hospital, then on the edge of town, which opened in 1942 and closed in 1946. On the site they founded a new Catholic college, St. Michael's College. Small portions of the eastern end of the old Bruns Army Hospital was purchased by the City of Santa Fe and the Santa Fe School District and used to build La Farge Library, which opened in 1978, and DeVargas Middle School.

In 1966 the college changed its name to College of Santa Fe. The school was run entirely by the Brothers and reached the peak of its success in the late '60s and early '70s with enrollment of 1,300 students. Enrollment went into a slow decline and in 2009 the college was sold to the city of Santa Fe, which in turn leased it to Laureate Education. In 2010 Laureate changed the name of the college to Santa Fe University of Art and Design.

CORDOVA ROAD

In 1883 the state legislature passed a law providing for construction of a penitentiary in Santa Fe. In 1884 it was built on what was then the edge of town, on Pen Road (short for Penitentiary Road), near the northeast corner of the present day intersection of Cordova Road and St. Francis Drive. Today two state office buildings, the Joseph Montoya building and the Harold Runnels building, occupy the site. By the 1950s, the prison was no longer on the edge of town. It was surrounded by houses and stores. The state legislature authorized construction of a new state penitentiary 15 miles to the south, and in 1956 it opened. In 1956 the old state pen was abandoned. But a portion of Pen (Penitentiary) Road still exists, just a few hundred yards long from St. Francis Drive to Cordova Road.

Coronado Center, the strip mall on Cordova where Trader Joe's is located, opened in 1964. Furr's Cafeteria has been in the mall since the mall's opening day. The site of Trader Joe's was originally a Furr's Supermarket. Coronado Center was built to attach to an older building at its eastern end. That building had, in its basement, a bowling alley called Coronado Lanes, and in its ground floor, the Coronado Twin movie theater. The bowling alley had opened in 1957. The bowling alley and theater closed in 1993 and the site became Leishman's furniture store.

The Whole Foods grocery store on St. Francis was originally a Safeway grocery store that opened in 1991. In the mid-1990s it became a Wild Oats natural foods grocery store. Whole Foods acquired the Wild Oats company in 2007 but this store's exterior signage did not change to say Whole Foods until 2010.

Salvador Perez recreation center, a municipal gym and swimming pool located a block north of Wild Oats, was built in 1954.

Body, a restaurant and yoga

studio on Cordova Road, opened in about 2003. Prior to that it had been vacant for three years. Originally the building was a Piggly Wiggly grocery store, which closed in the 1970s. The building became a Samon's appliance store, which closed in 1994. A health food grocery named Alfalfa's was in the building from 1995 to 2000.

10 Key Historic Events in Santa Fe History

- 1609--Founding of Santa Fe, as defined by the award of the status of a *villa* by the Spanish Crown, which ordered Pedro de Peralta to found Santa Fe with a plaza at its center.

- 1680--Pueblo Revolt. Enslaved Indians rebel against the Spanish, who fled to El Paso.

- 1692--Reconquest of Santa Fe by Don Diego de Vargas.

- 1821--Mexican Revolution. Mexico won independence from Spain in the spring but the news did not reach Santa Fe until September 11, 1821. The Mexican flag flies over the Palace of the Governors, from 1821 to 1846.

- 1846--During the Mexican-American War, Gen. Stephen Kearny leads 1,700 soldiers into New Mexico, finds Santa Fe undefended, and claims it for the U.S.

- 1848--Mexico and the U.S. sign the Treaty of Guadalupe Hildago, officially ending the Mexican-American War and ceding New Mexico and the southwest to the U.S.

-  1880--Arrival of the railroad.

- 1912--Unofficial beginning of Pueblo-Spanish Revival style.

- 1943--Los Alamos is founded, bringing people, commercial flights, traffic, secrecy, and money.

- 1957--Historical Zoning Ordinance is passed.

EPILOGUE

In the author's opinion, Santa Fe's heyday was the 1930s, the free-flowing decade when the rules were loose and loopy artists danced in the streets with shopkeepers, craftspeople and tourists. In the late 1940s, with the end of World War II, the automobile invaded and housing subdivisions arrived in dull grids.

The construction of semi-highways St. Francis Drive and St. Michael's Drive spelled the death of downtown. But the town remained wonderful until the 1970s, when second-home condos and K-Mart arrived. It went through a difficult period in the 1970s and '80s as legions of downtown shops closed. Happily, the Plaza area survived, while many downtowns across America have been killed by shopping malls.

Presently, Santa Fe is trying to balance historic preservation with the need to adapt to change. Pressure to loosen the Historic Styles Ordinance is growing, as the old Spanish-Pueblo Revival and Territorial styles have begun to look silly, like a parody of old Santa Fe. It's time to let the styles broaden, to allow square corners and different colors.

Santa Fe will thrive if it simultaneously preserves its past and allows change. Old, narrow streets should be preserved and illuminated electric signs should remain banned. Insufferable regulations that make it hard to open a business should be relaxed. Dull state office buildings, especially those along the south side of the Santa Fe River, should be moved to the southern edge of town. That land would be better used for shops and houses, as it was in the old days. Cars should be banned from the Plaza and perhaps everywhere inside of Paseo de Peralta. Let bicycles and bicycle rickshaws rule downtown. Santa Fe would have a great downtown again.

For future editions of this book, readers may email corrections, additions, and comments to: streetsofsantafe@live.com.

Footnotes

1. Quoted in "Faith in the City of Holy Faith," October 2010, La Herencia, *Santa Fe 400th Anniversary*.

2. Quoted from www.HHandR.com, the website of Heritage Hotels and Resorts, July 2009.

3. A book on the history of the school and chapel, called *Loretto: The Sisters and their Santa Fe Chapel*, was published in 2002.

4. The history of the Allison-James School was described in detail in *La Herencia*, winter 2007, vol. 56.

5. A detailed history of the house was described in "Historic Witter Bynner House on the Market" in the November 2008 real estate guide in *The New Mexican*.

6. Quoted in *The Food of Santa Fe*, Periplus Editions (HK) Ltd., by Dave DeWitt, 2000.

7. A detailed history of the building that housed the Second Ward School was published in the June/July 1977 bulletin of the Historic Santa Fe Foundation.

8. "Drive-in pioneer ran iconic '60s S.F. hangout," *The New Mexican*, December 14, 2010.

REFERENCES

Books

- Cook, Mary J. Straw. *Loretto: The Sisters and their Santa Fe Chapel*. Museum of New Mexico Press, Santa Fe, 2002.

- Cook, Mary J. Straw. *Doña Tules: Santa Fe's Courtesan and Gambler*, University of New Mexico Press, Albuquerque, 2007.

- Hammett, Kingsley. *Santa Fe: A Walk Through Time*. Gibbs Smith, Layton, Utah, 2004.

- Harrelson, Barbara. *Walks in Literary Santa Fe*. Gibbs Smith, Layton, Utah, 2007.

- La Farge, Oliver. *Santa Fe: The Autobiography of a Southwestern Town*. University of Oklahoma Press, Norman, Oklahoma, 1959.

- Levin, Eli. *Santa Fe Bohemia: The Art Colony, 1964 - 1980*. Sunstone Press, Santa Fe, 2006.

- Sherman, John. *Santa Fe: A Pictorial History*. Donning Co., Virginia Beach, Virginia, 1996.

- Tobias, Henry J. and Charles E. Woodhouse. *Santa Fe: A Modern History 1880 - 1990*, University of New Mexico Press, Albuquerque, 2001.

- Wilson, Chris. *The Myth of Santa Fe: Creating a Modern Regional Tradition*. University of New Mexico Press, Albuquerque, 1997.

Publications

- ☛ Archives of *The New Mexican*

- ☛ Newsletters of The New Mexico Jewish Historical Society.

- ☛ Bulletins of the Historic Santa Fe Foundation

- ☛ Street maps of the City of Santa Fe, published by the Chamber of Commerce, in 1949, 1953, 1959, 1973, 1974.

- ☛ 1952 and 1973 street maps of the City of Santa Fe, published by New Mexico State Highway Department.

Websites

- ☛ www.newmexicohistory.org

- ☛ www.palaceofthegovernors.org

- ☛ www.historicsantafe.org

- ☛ www.nmhistoricpreservation.org

- ☛ www.chefjohnnyvee.com

- ☛ www.compoundrestaurant.com

- ☛ www.santafewatershed.org

- ☛ www.amandakellerkonya.com

- ☛ www.santafecenterforappliedresearch.blogspot.com.

- ☛ www.peytonwright.com

Interviews

- ☞ Vint Blackwell, 4/19/08

- ☞ Maurice Bonal, 4/10/09

- ☞ Artie Garcia, 8/30/08

- ☞ Gerry Hopkins, 4/4/09

- ☞ John Kinsolving, 12/8/08

- ☞ Eli Levin, (now known as Jo Basiste), 3/15/09

- ☞ Diana MacArthur, 4/4/09

- ☞ Robert Spitz, 2/10/09

- ☞ Alexander Tschursin, 4/3/09

- ☞ Armand Ortega, 11/16/10

- ☞ Abe and Marian Silver, 5/19/09

Made in the USA
Lexington, KY
12 July 2012